朱生豪译文卷

A Midsummer Night's Dream

仲夏夜之梦

中英对照全译本

[英] 威廉·莎士比亚 著

William Shakespeare

朱生豪 译

世界图书出版公司

上海·西安·北京·广州

图书在版编目（CIP）数据

仲夏夜之梦：英汉对照 /（英）莎士比亚(Shakespeare,W.) 著；朱生豪译. -- 上海：上海世界图书出版公司, 2013.10（2015.2 重印）
ISBN 978-7-5100-6817-1

Ⅰ.①仲… Ⅱ.①莎… ②朱… Ⅲ.①英语－汉语－对照读物②喜剧－剧本－英国－中世纪 Ⅳ.①H319.4：I

中国版本图书馆 CIP 数据核字(2013)第 217293 号

仲夏夜之梦

[英] 威廉·莎士比亚 著
朱生豪 译

上海世界图书出版公司 出版发行
上海市广中路 88 号
邮政编码 200083
北京中科印刷有限公司印刷
如发现印刷质量问题，请与印刷厂联系
（电质检科话：010-84897777）
各地新华书店经销

开本：880×1230 1/32 印张：6.5 字数： 125 000
2015 年 2 月第 1 版第 2 次印刷
ISBN 978-7-5100-6817-1/H·1252
定价：19.80 元
http://www.wpcsh.com.cn
http://www.wpcsh.com

前　言

　　通过阅读文学名著学语言，是掌握英语的绝佳方法。既可接触原汁原味的英语，又能享受文学之美，一举两得，何乐不为？

　　对于喜欢阅读名著的读者，这是一个最好的时代，因为有成千上万的书可以选择；这又是一个不好的时代，因为在浩繁的卷帙中，很难找到适合自己的好书。

　　然而，你手中的这套丛书，值得你来信赖。

　　这套精选的中英对照名著全译丛书，未改编改写、未删节削减，且配有权威注释、部分书中还添加了精美插图。

　　要学语言、读好书，当读名著原文。如习武者切磋交流，同高手过招方能渐明其间奥妙，若一味在低端徘徊，终难登堂入室。积年流传的名著，就是书中"高手"。然而这个"高手"，却有真假之分。初读书时，常遇到一些挂了名著名家之名改写改编的版本，虽有助于了解基本情节，然而所得只是皮毛，你何曾真的就读过了那名著呢？一边是窖藏了50年的女儿红，一边是贴了女儿红标签的薄酒，那滋味，怎能一样？"朝闻道，夕死可矣。"人生短如朝露，当努力追求真正的美。

　　本套丛书还特别收录了十本朱生豪先生译著的莎士比亚戏剧，同样配有原著英文。朱生豪译本以"求于最大可能之范围内，保持原作之神韵"为宗旨，翻译考究、译笔流畅。他打破了莎士比亚写作的年代顺序，将戏剧分为喜剧、悲剧、史剧、杂剧四类编排，自成体系。本系列译文偶有异体字或旧译名，为方便读者理解，编者已一一加以注释。

　　读过本套丛书的原文全译，相信你会得书之真意、语言之精髓。

　　送君"开卷有益"之书，愿成文采斐然之人。

CONTENTS
目　录

A Midsummer Night's Dream

DRAMATIS PERSONAE

THESEUS, *duke of Athens*

EGEUS, *father to Hermia*

LYSANDER, *in love with Hermia*

DEMETRIUS, *in love with Hermia*

PHILOSTRATE, *master of the revels to Theseus*

QUINCE, *a carpenter*

SNUG, *a joiner*

BOTTOM, *a weaver*

FLUTE, *a bellows-mender*

SNOUT, *a tinker*

STARVELING, *a tailor*

HIPPOLYTA, *queen of the Amazons, betrothed to Theseus*

HERMIA, *daughter to Egeus, in love with Lysander*

HELENA, *in love with Demetrius*

OBERON, *king of the Fairies*

TITANIA, *queen of the Fairies*

PUCK, *or ROBIN GOODFELLOW, a fairy*

PEASBLOSSOM, *a fairy*

COBWEB, *a fairy*

MOTH, *a fairy*

MUSTARDSEED, *a fairy*

Other Fairies attending their King and Queen.

Attendants on Theseus and Hippolyta

剧中人物

忒修斯，雅典公爵

伊吉斯，赫米娅之父

拉山德，同恋赫米娅

狄米特律斯，同恋赫米娅

菲劳斯特莱特，忒修斯的掌戏乐之官

昆斯，木匠

斯纳格，细工木匠

波顿，织工

弗鲁特，修风箱者

斯诺特，补锅匠

斯塔佛林，裁缝

希波吕忒，阿玛宗女王，忒修斯之未婚妻

赫米娅，伊吉斯之女，恋拉山德

海丽娜，恋狄米特律斯

奥布朗，仙王

提泰妮娅，仙后

迫克，又名好人儿罗宾

豆花，小神仙

蛛网，小神仙

飞蛾，小神仙

芥子，小神仙

其他侍奉仙王仙后的小仙人们

忒修斯及希波吕忒的侍从

SCENE

Athens, and a wood not far from it

地点

雅典及附近的森林

ACT I SCENE I

Athens. The palace of Theseus.
[*Enter Theseus, Hippolyta, Philostrate, and Attendants.*]

THESEUS.   Now, fair Hippolyta, our nuptial hour
    Draws on apace; four happy days bring in
    Another moon; but, O, methinks, how slow
    This old moon wanes! She lingers my desires,
    Like to a step-dame or a dowager,
    Long withering out a young man's revenue.
HIPPOLYTA.   Four days will quickly steep themselves in nights;
    Four nights will quickly dream away the time;
    And then the moon, like to a silver bow
    New-bent in heaven, shall behold the night
    Of our solemnities.
THESEUS.   Go, Philostrate,
    Stir up the Athenian youth to merriments;
    Awake the pert and nimble spirit of mirth;
    Turn melancholy forth to funerals;
    The pale companion is not for our pomp.
    [*Exit Philostrate.*]
    Hippolyta, I wooed thee with my sword,

第一幕 第一场

雅典。忒修斯[1]宫中。

（忒修斯、希波吕忒、菲劳斯特莱特及侍从等上。）

忒修斯： 美丽的希波吕忒，现在我们的婚期已快要临近了，再过
四天幸福的日子，新月便将出来；但是唉！这个旧的月亮消逝
得多么慢，她耽延了我的希望，像一个老而不死的后母或寡妇，
尽是消耗着年轻人的财产。

希波吕忒： 四个白昼很快地便将成为黑夜，四个黑夜很快地可以
在梦中消度过去，那时月亮便将像新弯的银弓一样，在天上临
视我们的良宵。

忒修斯： 去，菲劳斯特莱特，激起雅典青年们的欢笑的心情，唤
醒了活泼的快乐精神，把忧愁驱到坟墓里去；那个脸色惨白的
家伙，是不应该让他参加在我们的结婚行列中的。（菲劳斯特
莱特下。）希波吕忒，我用我的剑向你求婚，用威力的侵凌赢
得了你的芳心；但这次我要换一个调子，我将用豪华、夸耀和
狂欢来举行我们的婚礼。

---

[1] 忒修斯（Theseus），今译提修斯，希腊神话里的雅典王子，统一了阿提卡半岛。

And won thy love doing thee injuries;

But I will wed thee in another key,

[*Enter Egeus, and his daughter Hermia, Lysander and Demetrius.*]

EGEUS.   Happy be Theseus, our renowned Duke!

THESEUS.   Thanks, good Egeus; what's the news with thee?

EGEUS.   Full of vexation come I, with complaint

Against my child, my daughter Hermia.

Stand forth, Demetrius. My noble lord,

This man hath my consent to marry her.

Stand forth, Lysander. And, my gracious Duke,

This man hath bewitched the bosom of my child.

Thou, thou, Lysander, thou hast given her rhymes,

And interchanged love-tokens with my child;

Thou hast by moonlight at her window sung,

With feigning voice, verses of feigning love,

And stol'n the impression of her fantasy

With bracelets of thy hair, rings, gawds, conceits,

Knacks, trifles, nosegays, sweetmeats – messengers

Of strong prevailment in unhardened youth;

With cunning hast thou filched my daughter's heart;

Turned her obedience, which is due to me,

To stubborn harshness. And, my gracious Duke,

Be it so she will not here before your Grace

Consent to marry with Demetrius,

（伊吉斯、赫米娅、拉山德、狄米特律斯上。）

伊吉斯：　威名远播的忒修斯公爵，祝您幸福！

忒修斯：　谢谢你，善良的伊吉斯。你有什么事情？

伊吉斯：　我怀着满心的气恼，来控诉我的孩子，我的女儿赫米娅。
走上前来，狄米特律斯。殿下，这个人，是我答应把我女儿嫁
给他的。走上前来，拉山德。殿下，这个人引诱坏了我的孩子。
你，你，拉山德，你写诗句给我的孩子，和她交换着爱情的纪
念物；你在月夜到她的窗前用做作的声调歌唱着假作多情的诗
篇；你用头发编成的腕环、戒指、虚华的饰物、琐碎的玩具、
花束、糖果——这些可以强烈地骗诱一个稚嫩的少女之心的
"信使"来偷得她的痴情；你用诡计盗取了她的心，煽惑她使
她对我的顺从变成倔强的顽抗。殿下，假如她现在当着您的面
仍旧不肯嫁给狄米特律斯，我就要要求雅典自古相传的权利，
因为她是我的女儿，我可以随意处置她；按照我们的法律，逢
到这样的情况，她要是不嫁给这位绅士，便应当立时处死。

I beg the ancient privilege of Athens:

As she is mine I may dispose of her;

Which shall be either to this gentleman

Or to her death, according to our law

Immediately provided in that case.

THESEUS. What say you, Hermia? Be advised, fair maid.

To you your father should be as a god;

One that composed your beauties; yea, and one

To whom you are but as a form in wax,

By him imprinted, and within his power

To leave the figure, or disfigure it.

Demetrius is a worthy gentleman.

HERMIA. So is Lysander.

In himself he is;

THESEUS. But, in this kind, wanting your father's voice,

The other must be held the worthier.

HERMIA. I would my father looked but with my eyes.

THESEUS. Rather your eyes must with his judgment look.

HERMIA. I do entreat your Grace to pardon me.

I know not by what power I am made bold,

Nor how it may concern my modesty

In such a presence here to plead my thoughts;

But I beseech your Grace that I may know

The worst that may befall me in this case,

If I refuse to wed Demetrius.

THESEUS. Either to die the death, or to abjure

忒修斯：　你有什么话说，赫米娅？当心一点吧，美貌的姑娘！你
　　　　的父亲对于你应当是一尊神明；你的美貌是他给予的，你就像
　　　　在他手中捏成的一块蜡像，他可以保全你，也可以毁灭你。狄
　　　　米特律斯是一个很好的绅士呢。

赫米娅：　拉山德也很好啊。

忒修斯：　他本人当然很好；但是要做你的丈夫，如果不能得到你
　　　　父亲的同意，那么比起来他就要差一筹了。

赫米娅：　我真希望我的父亲和我有同样的看法。

忒修斯：　实在还是你应该依从你父亲的看法才对。

赫米娅：　请殿下宽恕我！我不知道是什么一种力量使我如此大胆，
　　　　也不知道在这里披诉我的心思将会怎样影响到我的美名，但是
　　　　我要敬问殿下，要是我拒绝嫁给狄米特律斯，就会有什么最恶
　　　　的命运临到我的头上？

忒修斯：　不是受死刑，便是永远和男人隔绝。因此，美丽的赫米

For ever the society of men.

Therefore, fair Hermia, question your desires,

Know of your youth, examine well your blood,

Whether, if you yield not to your father's choice,

You can endure the livery of a nun,

For aye to be in shady cloister mewed,

To live a barren sister all your life,

Chanting faint hymns to the cold fruitless moon.

Thrice blessed they that master so their blood

To undergo such maiden pilgrimage;

But earthlier happy is the rose distilled

Than that which, withering on the virgin thorn

Grows, lives, and dies, in single blessedness.

HERMIA.   So will I grow, so live, so die, my lord,

Ere I will yield my virgin patent up

Unto his lordship, whose unwished yoke

My soul consents not to give sovereignty.

THESEUS.   Take time to pause; and by the next new moon –

The sealing-day betwixt my love and me

For everlasting bond of fellowship –

Upon that day either prepare to die

For disobedience to your father's will,

Or else to wed Demetrius, as he would,

Or on Diana's altar to protest

For aye austerity and single life.

DEMETR.   Relent, sweet Hermia; and, Lysander, yield

娅，仔细问一问你自己的心愿吧！考虑一下你的青春，好好地估量一下你血脉中的搏动；倘然不肯服从你父亲的选择，想想看能不能披上尼姑的道服，终生幽闭在阴沉的庵院中，向着凄凉寂寞的明月唱着暗淡的圣歌，做一个孤寂的修道女了此一生？她们能这样抑制热情，到老保持处女的贞洁，自然应当格外受到上天的眷宠；但是结婚的女子有如被采下炼制过的玫瑰，香气留存不散，比之孤独地自开自谢，奄然朽腐的花儿，在尘俗的眼光看来，总是要幸福得多了。

赫米娅：　就让我这样自开自谢吧，殿下，我不愿意把我的贞操奉献给我心里并不敬服的人。

忒修斯：　回去仔细考虑一下。等到新月初生的时候——我和我的爱人缔结永久的婚约的一天——你必须作出决定，倘不是因为违抗你父亲的意志而准备一死，便是听从他而嫁给狄米特律斯；否则就得在狄安娜的神坛前立誓严守戒律，终身不嫁。

狄米特律斯：　悔悟吧，可爱的赫米娅！拉山德，放弃你那没有理

    Thy crazed title to my certain right.

LYSANDE.   You have her father's love, Demetrius;

    Let me have Hermia's; do you marry him.

EGEUS.   Scornful Lysander, true, he hath my love;

    And what is mine my love shall render him;

    And she is mine; and all my right of her

    I do estate unto Demetrius.

LYSANDE.   I am, my lord, as well derived as he,

    As well possessed; my love is more than his;

    My fortunes every way as fairly ranked,

    If not with vantage, as Demetrius';

    And, which is more than all these boasts can be,

    I am beloved of beauteous Hermia.

    Why should not I then prosecute my right?

    Demetrius, I'll avouch it to his head,

    Made love to Nedar's daughter, Helena,

    And won her soul; and she, sweet lady, dotes,

    Devoutly dotes, dotes in idolatry,

    Upon this spotted and inconstant man.

THESEUS.   I must confess that I have heard so much,

    And with Demetrius thought to have spoke thereof;

    But, being over-full of self-affairs,

    My mind did lose it. But, Demetrius, come;

    And come, Egeus; you shall go with me;

    I have some private schooling for you both.

    For you, fair Hermia, look you arm yourself

由的要求，不要再跟我确定了的权利抗争吧！

拉山德：　你已经得到她父亲的爱，狄米特律斯，让我保有着赫米娅的爱吧；你去跟她的父亲结婚好了。

伊吉斯：　无礼的拉山德！一点不错，我欢喜他，我愿意把属于我所有的给他；她是我的，我要把我在她身上的一切权利都授给狄米特律斯。

拉山德：　殿下，我和他出身一样好；我和他一样有钱；我的爱情比他深得多；我的财产即使不比狄米特律斯更多，也绝不会比他少；比起这些来更值得夸耀的是，美丽的赫米娅爱的是我。那么为什么我不能享有我的权利呢？讲到狄米特律斯，我可以当他的面宣布，他曾经向奈达的女儿海丽娜调过情，把她弄得神魂颠倒；那位可爱的姑娘还痴心地恋着他，把这个缺德的负心汉当偶像一样崇拜。

忒修斯：　的确我也听到过不少闲话，曾经想和狄米特律斯谈谈这件事；但是因为自己的事情太多，所以忘了。来，狄米特律斯；来，伊吉斯；你们两人跟我来，我有些私人的话要开导你们。你，美丽的赫米娅，好好准备着，丢开你的情思，依从你父亲的意志，否则雅典的法律将要把你处死，或者使你宣誓独身；我们没有法子变更这条法律。来，希波吕忒；怎样，我的爱人？狄米特律斯和伊吉斯，走吧；我必须差你们为我们的婚礼办些

To fit your fancies to your father's will,

Or else the law of Athens yields you up –

Which by no means we may extenuate –

To death, or to a vow of single life.

Come, my Hippolyta; what cheer, my love?

Demetrius, and Egeus, go along;

I must employ you in some business

Against our nuptial, and confer with you

Of something nearly that concerns yourselves.

EGEUS.   With duty and desire we follow you.

[*Exeunt all but lysander and hermia.*]

LYSANDE.   How now, my love! Why is your cheek so pale?

How chance the roses there do fade so fast?

HERMIA.   Belike for want of rain, which I could well

Beteem them from the tempest of my eyes.

LYSANDE.   Ay me! for aught that I could ever read,

Could ever hear by tale or history,

The course of true love never did run smooth;

But either it was different in blood –

HERMIA.   O cross! Too high to be enthralled to low.

LYSANDE.   Or else misgraffed in respect of years –

HERMIA.   O spite! too old to be engaged to young.

LYSANDE.   Or else it stood upon the choice of friends –

HERMIA.   O hell! to choose love by another's eyes.

事，还要跟你们商量一些和你们有点关系的事。

伊吉斯：　我们敢不欣然跟从殿下。

（除拉山德、赫米娅外均下。）

拉山德：　怎么啦，我的爱人！为什么你的脸颊这样惨白？你脸上的蔷薇怎么会凋谢得这样快？

赫米娅：　多半是因为缺少雨露，但我眼中的泪涛可以灌溉它们。

拉山德：　唉！我在书上读到的，在传说或历史中听到的，真正的爱情，所走的道路永远是崎岖多阻；不是因为血统的差异——

赫米娅：　不幸啊，尊贵的要向微贱者屈节臣服！

拉山德：　便是因为年龄上的悬殊——

赫米娅：　可憎啊，年老的要和年轻人发生关系！

拉山德：　或者因为信从了亲友们的选择——

赫米娅：　倒霉啊，选择爱人要依赖他人的眼光！

LYSANDE.   Or, if there were a sympathy in choice,

War, death, or sickness, did lay siege to it,

Making it momentary as a sound,

Swift as a shadow, short as any dream,

Brief as the lightning in the collied night

That, in a spleen, unfolds both heaven and earth,

And ere a man hath power to say 'Behold!'

The jaws of darkness do devour it up;

So quick bright things come to confusion.

HERMIA.   If then true lovers have ever crossed,

It stands as an edict in destiny.

Then let us teach our trial patience,

Because it is a customary cross,

As due to love as thoughts and dreams and sighs,

Wishes and tears, poor Fancy's followers.

LYSANDE.   A good persuasion; therefore, hear me, Hermia.

I have a widow aunt, a dowager

Of great revenue, and she hath no child –

From Athens is her house remote seven leagues –

And she respects me as her only son.

There, gentle Hermia, may I marry thee;

And to that place the sharp Athenian law

Cannot pursue us. If thou lovest me then,

Steal forth thy father's house to-morrow night;

And in the wood, a league without the town,

Where I did meet thee once with Helena

拉山德： 或者，即使彼此两情悦服，但战争、死亡或疾病却侵害着它，使它像一个声音、一片影子、一段梦、黑夜中的一道闪电那样短促，在一刹那间展现了天堂和地狱，但还来不及说一声"瞧啊！"黑暗早已张开口把它吞噬了。光明的事物，总是那样很快地变成了混沌。

赫米娅： 既然真心的恋人们永远要受磨折似乎已是一条命运的定律，那么让我们练习着忍耐吧；因为这种磨折，正和忆念、幻梦、叹息、希望和哭泣一样，都是可怜的爱情缺不了的随从者。

拉山德： 你说得很对。听我吧，赫米娅。我有一个寡居的伯母，很有钱，却没有儿女，她看待我就像亲生的独子一样。她的家离开雅典二十里路；温柔的赫米娅，我可以在那边和你结婚，雅典法律的利爪不能追及我们。要是你爱我，请你在明天晚上溜出你父亲的屋子，走到郊外三里路地方的森林里——我就是在那边遇见你和海丽娜一同庆祝五月节[1]的——我将在那面等你。

---

[1] 每年五月一日是英国的五月节，人们采集花朵与朝露，并用露水洗脸。

To do observance to a morn of May,

There will I stay for thee.

HERMIA.   My good Lysander!

I swear to thee by Cupid's strongest bow,

By his best arrow, with the golden head,

By the simplicity of Venus' doves,

By that which knitteth souls and prospers loves,

And by that fire which burned the Carthage Queen,

When the false Trojan under sail was seen,

By all the vows that ever men have broke,

In number more than ever women spoke,

In that same place thou hast appointed me,

To-morrow truly will I meet with thee.

LYSANDE.   Keep promise, love. Look, here comes Helena.

[*Enter Helena.*]

HERMIA.   God speed fair Helena! Whither away?

HELENA.   Call you me fair? That fair again unsay.

Demetrius loves your fair. O happy fair!

Your eyes are lode-stars and your tongue's sweet air

More tuneable than lark to shepherd's ear,

When wheat is green, when hawthorn buds appear.

Sickness is catching: O, were favour so,

Yours would I catch, fair Hermia, ere I go!

My ear should catch your voice, my eye your eye,

赫米娅：　我的好拉山德！凭着丘匹德的最坚强的弓，凭着他的金
　　　　镞的箭，凭着维纳斯的鸽子的纯洁，凭着那结合灵魂、祐祐爱
　　　　情的神力，凭着古代迦太基女王焚身的烈火，当她看见她那
　　　　负心的特洛亚人扬帆而去的时候，凭着一切男子所毁弃的约
　　　　誓——那数目是远超过于女子所曾说过的，我向你发誓，明天
　　　　一定会到你所指定的那地方和你相会。

拉山德：　愿你不要失约，情人。瞧，海丽娜来了。

（海丽娜上。）

赫米娅：　上帝保佑美丽的海丽娜！你到哪里去？
海丽娜：　你称我"美丽"吗？请你把那两个字收回了吧！狄米特
　　　　律斯爱着你的美丽；幸福的美丽啊！你的眼睛是两颗明星，你
　　　　的甜蜜的声音比之小麦青青、山楂蓓蕾的时节送入牧人耳中的
　　　　云雀之歌还要动听。疾病是能染人的；唉！要是美貌也能传染
　　　　的话，美丽的赫米娅，我但愿染上你的美丽：我要用我的耳朵
　　　　捕获你的声音，用我的眼睛捕获你的睇视，用我的舌头捕获你
　　　　那柔美的旋律。要是除了狄米特律斯之外，整个世界都是属于
　　　　我所有，我愿意把一切捐弃，但求化身为你。啊！教给我怎样

My tongue should catch your tongue's sweet melody.

Were the world mine, Demetrius being bated,

The rest I'll give to be to you translated.

O, teach me how you look, and with what art

You sway the motion of Demetrius' heart!

HERMIA.　　I frown upon him, yet he loves me still.

HELENA.　　O that your frowns would teach my smiles such skill!

HERMIA.　　I give him curses, yet he gives me love.

HELENA.　　O that my prayers could such affection move!

HERMIA.　　The more I hate, the more he follows me.

HELENA.　　The more I love, the more he hateth me.

HERMIA.　　His folly, Helena, is no fault of mine.

HELENA.　　None, but your beauty; would that fault were mine!

HERMIA.　　Take comfort: he no more shall see my face;

Lysander and myself will fly this place.

Before the time I did Lysander see,

Seemed Athens as a paradise to me.

O, then, what graces in my love do dwell,

That he hath turned a heaven unto a hell!

LYSANDE.　　Helen, to you our minds we will unfold:

To-morrow night, when Phoebe doth behold

Her silver visage in the watery glass,

Decking with liquid pearl the bladed grass,

A time that lovers' flights doth still conceal,

Through Athens' gates have we devised to steal.

HERMIA.　　And in the wood where often you and I

流转眼波，用怎么一种魔力操纵着狄米特律斯的心？

赫米娅：	我向他皱着眉头，但是他仍旧爱我。
海丽娜：	唉，要是你的颦蹙能把那种本领传授给我的微笑就好了！
赫米娅：	我给他咒骂，但他给我爱情。
海丽娜：	唉，要是我的祈祷也能这样引动他的爱情就好了！
赫米娅：	我越是恨他，他越是跟随着我。
海丽娜：	我越是爱他，他越是讨厌我。
赫米娅：	海丽娜，他的傻并不是我的错。
海丽娜：	但那是你的美貌的错处；要是那错处是我的就好了！
赫米娅：	宽心吧，他不会再见我的脸了；拉山德和我将要逃开此地。在我不曾遇见拉山德之前，雅典对于我就像是一座天堂；啊，我的爱人身上，存在着一种多么神奇的力量，竟能把天堂变成一座地狱！

拉山德：　海丽娜，我们不愿瞒你。明天夜里，当月亮在镜波中反映她的银色的容颜、晶莹的露珠点缀在草叶尖上的时候——那往往是情奔最适当的时候，我们预备溜出雅典的城门。

赫米娅：　我的拉山德和我将要相会在林中，就是你我常常在那边

Upon faint primrose beds were wont to lie,

Emptying our bosoms of their counsel sweet,

There my Lysander and myself shall meet;

And thence from Athens turn away our eyes,

To seek new friends and stranger companies.

Farewell, sweet playfellow: pray thou for us,

And good luck grant thee thy Demetrius!

Keep word, Lysander: we must starve our sight

From lovers' food till morrow deep midnight.

LYSANDE.   I will, my Hermia.

[*Exit Hermia.*]

Helena, adieu;

As you on him, Demetrius dote on you.

[*Exit.*]

HELENA.   How happy some o'er other some can be!

Through Athens I am thought as fair as she.

But what of that? Demetrius thinks not so;

He will not know what all but he do know.

And as he errs, doting on Hermia's eyes,

So I, admiring of his qualities.

Things base and vile, holding no quantity,

Love can transpose to form and dignity.

Love looks not with the eyes, but with the mind;

And therefore is winged Cupid painted blind.

Nor hath Love's mind of any judgment taste;

Wings and no eyes figure unheedy haste;

淡雅的樱草花的花坛上躺着彼此吐露柔情的衷曲的所在,从那里我们便将离别雅典,去访寻新的朋友,和陌生人做伴了。再会吧,亲爱的游侣!请你为我们祈祷;愿你重新得到狄米特律斯的心!不要失约,拉山德;我们现在必须暂时忍受一下离别的痛苦,到明晚夜深时再见面吧!

拉山德: 一定的,我的赫米娅。(赫米娅下。)海丽娜,别了;如同你恋着他一样,但愿狄米特律斯也恋着你!(下。)

海丽娜: 有些人比起其他的人来是多么幸福!在全雅典大家都认为我跟她一样美;但那有什么相干呢?狄米特律斯是不这么认为的;除了他一个人之外大家都知道的事情,他不会知道。正如他那样错误地迷恋着赫米娅的秋波一样,我也是只知道爱慕他的才智;一切卑劣的弱点,在恋爱中都成为无足重轻,而变成美满和庄严。爱情是不用眼睛而用心灵看着的,因此生着翅膀的丘匹德常被描成盲目;而且爱情的判断全然没有理性,光有翅膀,不生眼睛,一味表示出鲁莽的急躁,因此爱神便据说是一个孩儿,因为在选择方面他常会弄错。正如顽皮的孩子惯爱发假誓一样,司爱情的小儿也到处赌着口不应心的咒。狄米特律斯在没有看见赫米娅之前,也曾像下雹一样发着誓,说他是完全属于我的,但这阵冰雹一感到身上的一丝热力,便立刻

And therefore is Love said to be a child,

Because in choice he is so oft beguiled.

As waggish boys in game themselves forswear,

So the boy Love is perjured everywhere;

For ere Demetrius looked on Hermia's eyne,

He hailed down oaths that he was only mine;

And when this hail some heat from Hermia felt,

So he dissolved, and showers of oaths did melt.

I will go tell him of fair Hermia's flight;

Then to the wood will he to-morrow night

Pursue her; and for this intelligence

If I have thanks, it is a dear expense.

But herein mean I to enrich my pain,

To have his sight thither and back again.

[*Exit.*]

溶解了，无数的盟言都化为乌有。我要去告诉他美丽的赫米娅的出奔；他知道了以后，明夜一定会到林中去追寻她。如果为着这次的通报消息，我能得到一些酬谢，我的代价也一定不小；但我的目的是要补报我的苦痛，使我能再一次聆接他的音容。（下。）

ACT I　SCENE II

Athens. Quince's house.

[*Enter Quince, Snug, Bottom, Flute, Snout, and Starveling.*]

QUINCE.　Is all our company here?

BOTTOM.　You were best to call them generally, man by man, according to the scrip.

QUINCE.　Here is the scroll of every man's name which is thought fit, through all Athens, to play in our interlude before the Duke and the Duchess on his wedding-day at night.

BOTTOM.　First, good Peter Quince, say what the play treats on; then read the names of the actors; and so grow to a point.

QUINCE.　Marry, our play is the most Lamentable Comedy and most Cruel Death of Pyramus and Thisbe.

BOTTOM.　A very good piece of work, I assure you, and a merry. Now, good Peter Quince, call forth your actors by the scroll. Masters, spread yourselves.

QUINCE.　Answer, as I call you. Nick Bottom, the weaver.

BOTTOM.　Ready. Name what part I am for, and proceed.

QUINCE.　You, Nick Bottom, are set down for Pyramus.

BOTTOM.　What is Pyramus? A lover, or a tyrant?

QUINCE.　A lover, that kills himself most gallant for love.

BOTTOM.　That will ask some tears in the true performing of it.If I

第一幕　第二场

同前。昆斯家中。

（昆斯、斯纳格、波顿、弗鲁特、斯诺特，斯塔佛林上。）

昆斯：　咱们一伙人都到了吗？

波顿：　你最好照着名单一个儿一个儿拢总地点一下名。

昆斯：　这儿是每个人名字都在上头的名单，整个雅典都承认，在
　　　　公爵跟公爵夫人结婚那晚上当着他们的面前扮演咱们这一出
　　　　插戏，这张名单上的弟兄们是再合适也没有的了。

波顿：　第一，好彼得·昆斯，说出来这出戏讲的是什么，然后再
　　　　把扮戏的人名字念出来，好有个头脑。

昆斯：　好，咱们的戏名是《最可悲的喜剧，以及皮拉摩斯和提斯
　　　　柏的最残酷的死》。

波顿：　那一定是篇出色的东西，咱可以担保，而且是挺有趣的。
　　　　现在，好彼得·昆斯，照着名单把你的角儿们的名字念出来吧。
　　　　列位，大家站开。

昆斯：　咱一叫谁的名字，谁就答应。尼克·波顿，织布的。

波顿：　有。先说咱应该扮哪一个角儿，然后再挨次叫下去。

昆斯：　你，尼克·波顿，派着扮皮拉摩斯。

波顿：　皮拉摩斯是谁呀？一个情郎呢，还是一个霸王？

昆斯：　是一个情郎，为着爱情的缘故，他挺勇敢地把自己毁了。

波顿：　要是演得活龙活现，那还得掉下几滴泪来。要是咱演起来

do it, let the audience look to their eyes; I will move storms; I will condole in some measure. To the rest – yet my chief humour is for a tyrant. I could play Ercles rarely, or a part to tear a cat in, to make all split.

'The raging rocks

And shivering shocks

Shall break the locks

Of prison gates;

And Phibbus' car

Shall shine from far,

And make and mar

The foolish Fates.'

This was lofty. Now name the rest of the players.

This is Ercles' vein, a tyrant's vein: a lover is more condoling.

QUINCE.   Francis Flute, the bellows-mender.

FLUTE.   Here, Peter Quince.

QUINCE.   Flute, you must take Thisbe on you.

FLUTE.   What is Thisbe? A wandering knight?

QUINCE.   It is the lady that Pyramus must love.

FLUTE.   Nay, faith, let not me play a woman; I have a beard coming.

QUINCE.   That's all one; you shall play it in a mask, and you may speak as small as you will.

BOTTOM.   An I may hide my face, let me play Thisbe too.

I'll speak in a monstrous little voice:

– 'Thisne, Thisne!'

–'Ah Pyramus, my lover dear! Thy Thisbe dear, and lady dear!'

的话，让看客们大家留心着自个儿的眼睛吧；咱要叫全场痛哭流涕，管保风云失色。把其余的人叫下去吧。但是扮霸王挺适合咱的胃口了。咱会把厄剌克勒斯扮得非常好，或者什么吹牛的角色，管保吓破了人的胆。

> 山岳狂怒的震动，
> 裂开了牢狱的门；
> 太阳在远方高升，
> 慑伏了神灵的魂。

那真是了不得！现在把其余的名字念下去吧。这是厄剌克勒斯的神气，霸王的神气；情郎还得忧愁一点。

昆斯：　法兰西斯·弗鲁特，修风箱的。

弗鲁特：　有，彼得·昆斯。

昆斯：　你得扮提斯柏。

弗鲁特：　提斯柏是谁呀？一个游行的侠客吗？

昆斯：　那是皮拉摩斯必须爱上的姑娘。

弗鲁特：　哦，真的，别叫咱扮一个娘儿们；咱的胡子已经长起来啦。

昆斯：　那没有问题；你得套上假脸扮演，你可以小着声音讲话。

波顿：　咱也可以把脸孔罩住，提斯柏也让咱来扮吧。咱会细声细气地说话，"提斯妮！提斯妮！""啊呀！皮拉摩斯，奴的情哥哥，是你的提斯柏，你的亲亲爱爱的姑娘！"

QUINCE.　No, no, you must play Pyramus; and, Flute, you Thisbe.

BOTTOM.　Well, proceed.

QUINCE.　Robin Starveling, the tailor.

STARV.　Here, Peter Quince.

QUINCE.　Robin Starveling, you must play Thisbe's mother.

Tom Snout, the tinker.

SNOUT.　Here, Peter Quince.

QUINCE.　You, Pyramus' father; myself, Thisbe's father;

Snug, the joiner, you, the lion's part. And, I hope, here is a play fitted.

SNUG.　Have you the lion's part written? Pray you, if it be, give it me, for I am slow of study.

QUINCE.　You may do it extempore, for it is nothing but roaring.

BOTTOM.　Let me play the lion too. I will roar that I will do any man's heart good to hear me; I will roar that I will make the Duke say Let him roar again, let him roar again.

QUINCE.　An you should do it too terribly, you would fright the Duchess and the ladies, that they would shriek; and that were enough to hang us all.

ALL.　That would hang us, every mother's son.

BOTTOM.　I grant you, friends, if you should fright the ladies out of their wits, they would have no more discretion but to hang us; but I will aggravate my voice so, that I will roar you as gently as any sucking dove; I will roar you an 'twere any nightingale.

QUINCE.　You can play no part but Pyramus; for Pyramus is a sweet-faced man; a proper man, as one shall see in a summer's

昆斯：　不行，不行，你必须扮皮拉摩斯。弗鲁特，你必须扮提斯柏。

波顿：　好吧，叫下去。

昆斯：　罗宾·斯塔佛林，当裁缝的。

斯塔佛林：　有，彼得·昆斯。

昆斯：　罗宾·斯塔佛林，你扮提斯柏的母亲。汤姆·斯诺特，补锅子的。

斯诺特：　有，彼得·昆斯。

昆斯：　你扮皮拉摩斯的爸爸；咱自己扮提斯柏的爸爸；斯纳格，做细木工的，你扮一只狮子：咱想这本戏就此分配好了。

斯纳格：　你有没有把狮子的台词写下？要是有的话，请你给我，因为我记性不大好。

昆斯：　你不用预备，你只要嚷嚷就算了。

波顿：　让咱也扮狮子吧。咱会嚷嚷，叫每一个人听见了都非常高兴；咱会嚷着嚷着，连公爵都传下谕旨来说，"让他再嚷下去吧！让他再嚷下去吧！"

昆斯：　你要嚷得那么可怕，吓坏了公爵夫人和各位太太小姐们，吓得她们尖声叫起来；那准可以把咱们一起给吊死了。

众人：　那准会把咱们一起给吊死，每一个母亲的儿子都逃不了。

波顿：　朋友们，你们说的很是；要是你把太太们吓昏了头，她们一定会不顾三七二十一把咱们给吊死。但是咱可以把声音压得高一些，不，提得低一些；咱会嚷得就像一只吃奶的小鸽子那么的温柔，嚷得就像一只夜莺。

昆斯：　你只能扮皮拉摩斯；因为皮拉摩斯是一个讨人欢喜的小白脸，一个体面人，就像你可以在夏天看到的那种人；他又是一

day; a most lovely gentleman-like man; therefore you must needs play Pyramus.

BOTTOM.   Well, I will undertake it. What beard were I best to play it in?

QUINCE.   Why, what you will.

BOTTOM.   I will discharge it in either your straw-colour beard, your orange-tawny beard, your purple-in-grain beard you're your French-crown-colour beard, your perfect yellow.

QUINCE.   Some of your French crowns have no hair at all, and then you will play bare-faced. But, masters, here are your parts; and I am to entreat you, request you, and desire you, to con them by to-morrow night; and meet me in the palace wood, a mile without the town, by moonlight; there will we rehearse; for if we meet in the city, we shall be dogged with company, and our devices known. In the meantime I will draw a bill of properties, such as our play wants. I pray you, fail me not.

BOTTOM.   We will meet; and there we may rehearse most obscenely and courageously. Take pains; be perfect; adieu.

QUINCE.   At the Duke's oak we meet.

BOTTOM.   Enough; hold, or cut bow-strings.

[*Exeunt.*]

个可爱的堂堂绅士模样的人；因此你必须扮皮拉摩斯。

波顿：　行，咱就扮皮拉摩斯。顶好咱挂什么须？

昆斯：　那随你便吧。

波顿：　咱可以挂你那稻草色的须，你那橙黄色的须，你那紫红色的须，或者你那法国金洋钱色的须，纯黄色的须。

昆斯：　你还是光着脸蛋吧。列位，这儿是你们的台词。咱请求你们，恳求你们，要求你们，在明儿夜里念熟，趁着月光，在郊外一里路地方的森林里咱们碰头，在那边咱们要排练排练；因为要是咱们在城里排练，就会有人跟着咱们，咱们的玩意儿就要泄漏出去。同时咱要开一张咱们演戏所需要的东西的单子。请你们大家不要误事。

波顿：　咱们一定在那边碰头；咱们在那边排练起来可以像样点儿，胆大点儿。大家辛苦干一下，要干得非常好。再会吧。

昆斯：　咱们在公爵的橡树底下再见。

波顿：　好了，可不许失约。（同下。）

ACT II SCENE I

A wood near Athens.

[Enter a Fairy at One door, and Puck at another.]

PUCK.   How now, spirit! whither wander you?

FAIRY.   Over hill, over dale,

    Thorough bush, thorough brier,

    Over park, over pale,

    Thorough flood, thorough fire,

    I do wander every where,

    Swifter than the moon's sphere;

    And I serve the Fairy Queen,

    To dew her orbs upon the green.

    The cowslips tall her pensioners be;

    In their gold coats spots you see;

    Those be rubies, fairy favours,

    In those freckles live their savours.

    I must go seek some dewdrops here,

    And hang a pearl in every cowslip's ear.

    Farewell, thou lob of spirits; I'll be gone.

    Our Queen and all her elves come here anon.

PUCK.   The King doth keep his revels here to-night;

    Take heed the Queen come not within his sight;

第二幕　第一场

雅典附近的森林。

（一小仙及迫克自相对方向上。）

迫克：　喂，精灵！你飘流到哪里去？

小仙：　越过了溪谷和山陵，

　　　　穿过了荆棘和丛薮，

　　　　越过了围场和园庭，

　　　　穿过了激流和熛火：

　　　　我在各地漂游流浪，

　　　　轻快得像是月亮光；

　　　　我给仙后奔走服务，

　　　　草环上缀满轻轻露。

　　　　亭亭的莲馨花是她的近侍，

　　　　黄金的衣上饰着点点斑痣；

　　　　那些是仙人们投赠的红玉，

　　　　中藏着一缕缕的芳香馥郁；

　　　　我要在这里访寻几滴露水，

　　　　给每朵花挂上珍珠的耳坠。

　　　　再会，再会吧，你粗野的精灵！

　　　　因为仙后的大驾快要来临。

迫克：　今夜大王在这里大开欢宴，

　　　　千万不要让他俩彼此相见；

For Oberon is passing fell and wrath,

Because that she as her attendant hath

A lovely boy, stolen from an Indian king.

She never had so sweet a changeling;

And jealous Oberon would have the child

Knight of his train, to trace the forests wild;

But she perforce withholds the loved boy,

Crowns him with flowers, and makes him all her joy.

And now they never meet in grove or green,

By fountain clear, or spangled starlight sheen,

But they do square, that all their elves for fear

Creep into acorn cups and hide them there.

FAIRY.   Either I mistake your shape and making quite,

Or else you are that shrewd and knavish sprite

Call'd Robin Goodfellow. Are not you he

That frights the maidens of the villagery;

Skim milk, and sometimes labour in the quern,

And bootless make the breathless housewife churn,

And sometime make the drink to bear no barm,

Mislead night-wanderers, laughing at their harm?

Those that Hobgoblin call you, and sweet Puck,

You do their work, and they shall have good luck.

Are not you he?

PUCK.   Thou speakest aright:

I am that merry wanderer of the night.

I jest to Oberon, and make him smile

奥布朗的脾气可不是顶好，

为着王后的固执十分着恼，

她偷到了一个印度小王子，

就像心肝一样怜爱和珍视；

奥布朗看见了有些儿眼红，

想要把他充作自己的侍童；

可是她哪里便肯把他割爱，

满头花朵她为他亲手插戴。

从此林中、草上、泉畔和月下，

他们一见面便要破口相骂；

小妖们往往吓得胆战心慌，

没命地钻向橡斗中间躲藏。

小仙：　要是我没有把你认错，你大概便是名叫罗宾好人儿的狡狯
　　　　的、淘气的精灵了。你就是惯爱吓唬乡村的女郎，在人家的牛
　　　　乳上撮去了乳脂，使那气喘吁吁的主妇整天也搅不出奶油来；
　　　　有时你暗中替人家磨谷，有时弄坏了酒使它不能发酵；夜里走
　　　　路的人，你把他们引入了迷路，自己却躲在一旁窃笑；谁叫你
　　　　"大仙"或是"好迫克"的，你就给他幸运，帮他做工：那就
　　　　是你吗？

迫克：　仙人，你说得正是；我就是那个快活的夜游者。我在奥布
　　　　朗跟前想出种种笑话来逗他发笑，看见一头肥胖精
　　　　我就学着雌马的嘶声把它迷昏了头；有时我化作一

When I a fat and bean-fed horse beguile,

Neighing in likeness of a filly foal;

And sometime lurk I in a gossip's bowl

In very likeness of a roasted crab,

And, when she drinks, against her lips I bob,

And on her withered dewlap pour the ale.

The wisest aunt, telling the saddest tale,

Sometime for three-foot stool mistaketh me;

Then slip I from her bum, down topples she,

And tailor cries, and falls into a cough;

And then the whole quire hold their hips and laugh,

And waxen in their mirth, and neeze, and swear

A merrier hour was never wasted there.

But room, fairy, here comes Oberon.

FAIRY.   And here my mistress. Would that he were gone!

[*Enter Oberon at one door, with his train, and Titania, at another, with hers.*]

OBERON.   Ill met by moonlight, proud Titania.

TITANIA.   What, jealous Oberon! Fairies, skip hence;

I have forsworn his bed and company.

OBERON.   Tarry, rash wanton; am not I thy lord?

TITANIA.   Then I must be thy lady; but I know

When thou hast stolen away from fairy land,

And in the shape of Corin sat all day,

苹果，躲在老太婆的酒碗里，等她举起碗想喝的时候，我就拍的弹到她嘴唇上，把一碗麦酒都倒在她那皱瘪的喉皮上；有时我化作三脚的凳子，满肚皮人情世故的婶婶刚要坐下来一本正经讲她的故事，我便从她的屁股底下滑走，把她翻了一个大元宝，一头喊"好家伙！"一头咳呛个不住，于是周围的人大家笑得前仰后合，他们越想越好笑，鼻涕眼泪都笑了出来，发誓说从来不曾逢到过比这更有趣的事。但是让开路来，仙人，奥布朗来了。

小仙：　娘娘也来了。他要是走开了才好！

（奥布朗及提泰妮娅各带侍从自相对方向上。）

奥布朗：　真不巧又在月光下碰见你，骄傲的提泰妮娅！

提泰妮娅：　嘿，嫉妒的奥布朗！神仙们，快快走开；我已经发誓不和他同游同寝了。

奥布朗：　等一等，坏脾气的女人！我不是你的夫君吗？

提泰妮娅：　那么我也一定是你的尊夫人了。但是你从前溜出了仙境，扮作牧人的样子，整天吹着麦笛，唱着情歌，向风骚的牧女调情，这种事我全知道。今番你为什么要从迢迢的印度平原

Playing on pipes of corn, and versing love

To amorous Phillida. Why art thou here,

Come from the farthest steep of India,

But that, forsooth, the bouncing Amazon,

Your buskined mistress and your warrior love,

To Theseus must be wedded, and you come

To give their bed joy and prosperity?

OBERON.　How canst thou thus, for shame, Titania,

Glance at my credit with Hippolyta,

Knowing I know thy love to Theseus?

Didst not thou lead him through the glimmering night

From Perigenia, whom he ravished?

And make him with fair Æglés break his faith,

With Ariadne and Antiopa?

TITANIA.　These are the forgeries of jealousy;

And never, since the middle summer's spring,

Met we on hill, in dale, forest, or mead,

By paved fountain, or by rushy brook,

Or in the beached margent of the sea,

To dance our ringlets to the whistling wind,

But with thy brawls thou hast disturbed our sport.

Therefore the winds, piping to us in vain,

As in revenge, have sucked up from the sea

Contagious fogs; which, falling in the land,

Hath every pelting river made so proud

That they have overborne their continents.

上赶到这里来呢？无非是为着那位身材高大的阿玛宗女王，你的穿靴子的爱人，要嫁给忒修斯了，所以你得来向他们道贺道贺。

奥布朗：　你怎么好意思说出这种话来，提泰妮娅，把我的名字和希波吕忒牵涉在一起侮蔑我？你自己知道你和忒修斯的私情瞒不过我。不是你在朦胧的夜里引导他离开被他所俘虏的佩丽古娜？不是你使他负心地遗弃了美丽的伊葛尔、爱丽亚邓和安提奥巴？

提泰妮娅：　这些都是因为嫉妒而捏造出来的谎话。自从仲夏之初，我们每次在山上、谷中、树林里、草场上、细石铺底的泉旁或是海滨的沙滩上聚集，预备和着鸣啸的风声跳环舞的时候，总是被你吵断我们的兴致。风因为我们不理会他的吹奏，生了气，便从海中吸起了毒雾；毒雾化成瘴雨下降地上，使每一条小小的溪河都耀武扬威地泛滥到岸上：因此牛儿白白牵着轭，农夫枉费了他的血汗，青青的嫩禾还没有长上芒须便腐烂了；空了的羊栏露出在一片汪洋的田中，乌鸦饱啖着瘟死了的羊群的尸体；跳舞作乐的草泥坂上满是湿泥，杂草乱生的曲径因为没有人行走，已经无法辨认。人们在五月天要穿冬季的衣服；晚上再听不到欢乐的颂歌。执掌潮汐的月亮，因为再也听不见夜间颂神的歌声，气得脸孔发白，在空气中播满了湿气，人一沾染

The ox hath therefore stretched his yoke in vain,

The ploughman lost his sweat, and the green corn

Hath rotted ere his youth attained a beard;

The fold stands empty in the drowned field,

And crows are fatted with the murrain flock;

The nine men's morris is filled up with mud,

And the quaint mazes in the wanton green,

For lack of tread, are undistinguishable.

The human mortals want their winter here;

No night is now with hymn or carol blest;

Therefore the moon, the governess of floods,

Pale in her anger, washes all the air,

That rheumatic diseases do abound.

And thorough this distemperature we see

The seasons alter: hoary-headed frosts

Fall in the fresh lap of the crimson rose;

And on old Hyem's thin and icy crown

An odorous chaplet of sweet summer buds

Is, as in mockery, set. The spring, the summer,

The childing autumn, angry winter, change

Their wonted liveries; and the mazed world,

By their increase, now knows not which is which.

And this same progeny of evils comes

From our debate, from our dissension;

We are their parents and original.

OBERON.　Do you amend it, then; it lies in you.

上就要害风湿症。因为天时不正，季候也反了常：白头的寒霜倾倒在红颜的蔷薇的怀里，年迈的冬神却在薄薄的冰冠上嘲讽似的缀上了夏天芬芳的蓓蕾的花环。春季、夏季、丰收的秋季、暴怒的冬季，都改换了他们素来的装束，惊愕的世界不能再凭着他们的出产辨别出谁是谁来。这都因为我们的不和所致，我们是一切灾祸的根源。

奥布朗：　那么你就该设法补救；这全然在你的手中。为什么提泰

Why should Titania cross her Oberon?

I do but beg a little changeling boy

To be my henchman.

TITANIA.　Set your heart at rest;

The fairy land buys not the child of me.

His mother was a vot'ress of my order;

And, in the spiced Indian air, by night,

Full often hath she gossiped by my side;

And sat with me on Neptune's yellow sands,

Marking the embarked traders on the flood;

When we have laughed to see the sails conceive,

And grow big-bellied with the wanton wind;

Which she, with pretty and with swimming gait

Following – her womb then rich with my young squire

Would imitate, and sail upon the land,

To fetch me trifles, and return again,

As from a voyage, rich with merchandise.

But she, being mortal, of that boy did die;

And for her sake do I rear up her boy;

And for her sake I will not part with him.

OBERON.　How long within this wood intend you stay?

TITANIA.　Perchance till after Theseus' wedding-day.

If you will patiently dance in our round,

And see our moonlight revels, go with us;

If not, shun me, and I will spare your haunts.

OBERON.　Give me that boy and I will go with thee.

妮娅要违拗她的奥布朗呢？我所要求的,不过是一个小小的换儿做我的侍童罢了。

提泰妮娅： 请你死了心吧,拿整个仙境也不能从我手里换得这个孩子。他的母亲是我神坛前的一个信徒,在芬芳的印度的夜里,她常常在我身旁闲谈,陪我坐在海边的黄沙上,凝望着海上的商船;我们一起笑着,看那些船帆因狂荡的风而怀孕,一个个凸起了肚皮;她那时正也怀孕着这个小宝贝,便学着船帆的样子,美妙而轻快地凌风而行,为我往岸上寻取各种杂物,回来时就像航海而归,带来了无数的商品。但她因为是一个凡人,所以在产下这孩子时便死了。为着她的缘故我才抚养她的孩子,也为着她的缘故我不愿舍弃他。

奥布朗： 你预备在这林中耽搁多少时候?

提泰妮娅： 也许要到忒修斯的婚礼以后。要是你肯耐心地和我们一起跳舞,看看我们月光下的游戏,那么跟我们一块儿走吧;不然的话,请你不要见我,我也决不到你的地方来。

奥布朗： 把那个孩子给我,我就和你一块儿走。

TITANIA.　Not for thy fairy kingdom. Fairies, away.

We shall chide downright if I longer stay.

[*Exit Titania with her train.*]

OBERON.　Well, go thy way; thou shalt not from this grove

Till I torment thee for this injury.

My gentle Puck, come hither. Thou remember'st

Since once I sat upon a promontory,

And heard a mermaid on a dolphin's back

Uttering such dulcet and harmonious breath

That the rude sea grew civil at her song,

And certain stars shot madly from their spheres

To hear the sea-maid's music.

PUCK.　I remember.

OBERON.　That very time I saw, but thou couldst not,

Flying between the cold moon and the earth

Cupid, all armed; a certain aim he took

At a fair vestal, throned by the west,

And loosed his love-shaft smartly from his bow,

As it should pierce a hundred thousand hearts;

But I might see young Cupid's fiery shaft

Quenched in the chaste beams of the watery moon;

And the imperial votaress passed on,

In maiden meditation, fancy-free.

Yet marked I where the bolt of Cupid fell.

提泰妮娅：　把你的仙国跟我掉换都别想。神仙们，去吧！要是我再多留一刻，我们就要吵起来了。

（提泰妮娅率侍从等下。）

奥布朗：　好，去你的吧！为着这次的侮辱，我一定要在你离开这座林子之前给你一些惩罚。我的好迫克，过来。你记不记得有一次我坐在一个海岬上，望见一个美人鱼骑在海豚的背上，她的歌声是这样婉转而谐美，镇静了狂暴的怒海，好几个星星都疯狂地跳出了它们的轨道，为了听这海女的音乐？

迫克：　我记得。

奥布朗：　就在那个时候，你看不见，但我能看见持着弓箭的丘匹德在冷月和地球之间飞翔；他瞄准了坐在西方宝座上的一个美好的童贞女，很灵巧地从他的弓上射出他的爱情之箭，好像它能刺透十万颗心的样子。可是只见小丘匹德的火箭在如水的冷洁的月光中熄灭，那位童贞的女王心中一尘不染，沉浸在纯洁的思念中安然无恙；但是我看见那支箭却落下在西方一朵小小的花上，那花本来是乳白色的，现在已因爱情的创伤而被染成紫色，少女们把它称作"爱懒花"。去给我把那花采来。我曾经给你看过它的样子；它的汁液如果滴在睡着的人的眼皮上，无论男女，醒来一眼看见什么生物，都会发疯似的对它恋爱。给我采这种花来；在鲸鱼还不曾游过三里路之前，必须回来复命。

It fell upon a little western flower,

Before milk-white, now purple with love's wound,

And maidens call it Love-in-idleness.

Fetch me that flow'r, the herb I showed thee once.

The juice of it on sleeping eyelids laid

Will make or man or woman madly dote

Upon the next live creature that it sees.

Fetch me this herb, and be thou here again

Ere the leviathan can swim a league.

PUCK.　I'll put a girdle round about the earth

In forty minutes.

[Exit Puck.]

OBERON.　Having once this juice,

I'll watch Titania when she is asleep,

And drop the liquor of it in her eyes;

The next thing then she waking looks upon,

Be it on lion, bear, or wolf, or bull,

On meddling monkey, or on busy ape,

She shall pursue it with the soul of love.

And ere I take this charm from off her sight,

As I can take it with another herb,

I'll make her render up her page to me.

But who comes here? I am invisible;

And I will overhear their conference.

[Enter Demetrius, Helena following him.]

迫克： 我可以在四十分钟内环绕世界一周。

（下。）

奥布朗： 这种花汁一到了手，我便留心着等提泰妮娅睡了的时候把它滴在她的眼皮上；她一醒来第一眼看见的东西，无论是狮子也好，熊也好，狼也好，公牛也好，或者好事的猕猴、忙碌的无尾猿也好，她都会用最强烈的爱情追求它。我可以用另一种草解去这种魔力，但第一我先要叫她把那个孩子让给我。可是谁到这儿来啦？凡人看不见我，让我听听他们的谈话。

（狄米特律斯上，海丽娜随其后。）

DEMETR.　I love thee not, therefore pursue me not.

Where is Lysander and fair Hermia?

The one I'll slay, the other slayeth me.

Thou told'st me they were stol'n unto this wood,

And here am I, and wood within this wood,

Because I cannot meet my Hermia.

Hence, get thee gone, and follow me no more.

HELENA.　You draw me, you hard-hearted adamant;

But yet you draw not iron, for my heart

Is true as steel. Leave you your power to draw,

And I shall have no power to follow you.

DEMETR.　Do I entice you? Do I speak you fair?

Or, rather, do I not in plainest truth

Tell you I do not nor I cannot love you?

HELENA.　And even for that do I love you the more.

I am your spaniel; and, Demetrius,

The more you beat me, I will fawn on you.

Use me but as your spaniel, spurn me, strike me,

Neglect me, lose me; only give me leave,

Unworthy as I am, to follow you.

What worser place can I beg in your love,

And yet a place of high respect with me,

Than to be used as you use your dog?

DEMETR.　Tempt not too much the hatred of my spirit;

For I am sick when I do look on thee.

HELENA.　And I am sick when I look not on you.

狄米特律斯：　我不爱你，所以别跟着我。拉山德和美丽的赫米娅在哪儿？我要把拉山德杀死，但我的命却悬在赫米娅手中。你对我说他们私奔到这座林子里，因此我赶到这儿来；可是因为遇不见我的赫米娅，我简直要在这林子里发疯啦。滚开！快走，不许再跟着我！

海丽娜：　是你吸引我跟着你的，你这硬心肠的磁石！可是你所吸的却不是铁，因为我的心像钢一样坚贞。要是你去掉你的吸引力，那么我也就没有力量再跟着你了。

狄米特律斯：　是我引诱你吗？我曾经向你说过好话吗？我不是曾经明明白白地告诉过你，我不爱你，而且也不能爱你吗？

海丽娜：　即使那样，也只是使我爱你爱得更加厉害。我是你的一条狗，狄米特律斯；你越是打我，我越是向你献媚。请你就像对待你的狗一样对待我吧，踢我、打我、冷淡我、不理我，都好，只容许我跟随着你，虽然我是这么不好。在你的爱情里我要求的地位还能比一条狗都不如吗？但那对于我已经是十分可贵了。

狄米特律斯：　不要过分惹起我的厌恨吧；我一看见你就头痛。

海丽娜：　可是我不看见你就心痛。

DEMETR.   You do impeach your modesty too much

To leave the city and commit yourself

Into the hands of one that loves you not;

To trust the opportunity of night,

And the ill counsel of a desert place,

With the rich worth of your virginity.

HELENA.   Your virtue is my privilege for that:It is not night when I

do see your face,

Therefore I think I am not in the night;

Nor doth this wood lack worlds of company,

For you, in my respect, are all the world.

Then how can it be said I am alone

When all the world is here to look on me?

DEMETR.   I'll run from thee and hide me in the brakes,

And leave thee to the mercy of wild beasts.

HELENA.   The wildest hath not such a heart as you.

Run when you will; the story shall be changed:

Apollo flies, and Daphne holds the chase;

The dove pursues the griffin; the mild hind

Makes speed to catch the tiger – bootless speed,

When cowardice pursues and valour flies.

DEMETR.   I will not stay thy questions; let me go;

Or, if thou follow me, do not believe

But I shall do thee mischief in the wood.

HELENA.   Ay, in the temple, in the town, the field,

You do me mischief. Fie, Demetrius!

狄米特律斯：　你太不顾虑你自己的体面了，竟擅自离开城中，把你自己交托在一个不爱你的人手里；你也不想想你的贞操多么值钱，就在黑夜中这么一个荒凉的所在盲目地听从着不可知的命运。

海丽娜：　你的德行使我安心这样做：因为当我看见你面孔的时候，黑夜也变成了白昼，因此我并不觉得现在是在夜里；你在我的眼里是整个世界，因此在这座林中我也不愁缺少伴侣：要是整个世界都在这儿瞧着我，我怎么还是单身独自一人呢？

狄米特律斯：　我要逃开你，躲在丛林之中，任凭野兽把你怎样处置。

海丽娜：　最凶恶的野兽也不像你那样残酷。你要逃开我就逃开吧；从此以后，古来的故事要改过了：逃走的是阿波罗，追赶的是达芙妮[1]；鸽子追逐着鹰隼；温柔的牝鹿追捕着猛虎；然而弱者追求勇者，结果总是徒劳无益的。

狄米特律斯：　我不高兴听你再唠叨下去。让我走吧；要是你再跟着我，相信我，在这座林中你要被我欺负的。

海丽娜：　嗯，在神庙中，在市镇上，在乡野里，你到处欺负我。

---

[1] 希腊罗马神话中，日神阿波罗（Apollo）爱慕仙女达芙妮（Daphne），达芙妮为了逃避他，而化为月桂树。

Your wrongs do set a scandal on my sex.

We cannot fight for love as men may do;

We should be wooed, and were not made to woo.

[*Exit Demetrius.*]

I'll follow thee, and make a heaven of hell,

To die upon the hand I love so well.

[*Exit Helena.*]

OBERON.　Fare thee well, nymph; ere he do leave this grove,

　　Thou shalt fly him, and he shall seek thy love.

[*Re-enter Puck.*]

OBERON.　Hast thou the flower there? Welcome, wanderer.

PUCK.　Ay, there it is.

OBERON.　I pray thee, give it me.

　　I know a bank where the wild thyme blows,

　　Where oxlips and the nodding violet grows,

　　Quite over-canopied with luscious woodbine,

　　With sweet musk-roses, and with eglantine;

　　There sleeps Titania sometime of the night,

　　Lulled in these flowers with dances and delight;

　　And there the snake throws her enamelled skin,

　　Weed wide enough to wrap a fairy in;

　　And with the juice of this I'll streak her eyes,

　　And make her full of hateful fantasies.

唉，狄米特律斯！你的虐待我已经使我们女子蒙上了耻辱。我们是不会像男人一样为爱情而争斗的；我们应该被人家求爱，而不是向人家求爱。（狄米特律斯下。）我要立意跟随你；我愿死在我所深爱的人的手中，好让地狱化为天宫。

（下。）

奥布朗：　再会吧，女郎！当他还没有离开这座树林，你将逃避他，他将追求你的爱情。

（迫克重上。）

奥布朗：　你已经把花采来了吗？欢迎啊，浪游者！
迫克：　是的，它就在这儿。
奥布朗：　请你把它给我。
　　　　我知道一处茴香盛开的水滩，
　　　　长满着樱草和盈盈的紫罗丝，
　　　　馥郁的金银花，芝泽的野蔷薇，
　　　　漫天张起了一幅芬芳的锦帷。
　　　　有时提泰妮娅在群花中酣醉，
　　　　柔舞清歌低低地抚着她安睡；
　　　　小花蛇在那里丢下发亮的皮，
　　　　小仙人拿来当做合身的外衣。
　　　　我要洒一点花汁在她的眼上，
　　　　让她充满了各种可憎的幻象。

Take thou some of it, and seek through this grove:

A sweet Athenian lady is in love

With a disdainful youth; anoint his eyes;

But do it when the next thing he espies

May be the lady. Thou shalt know the man

By the Athenian garments he hath on.

Effect it with some care, that he may prove

More fond on her than she upon her love.

And look thou meet me ere the first cock crow.

PUCK.　　Fear not, my lord; your servant shall do so.

　　[*Exeunt.*]

其余的你带了去在林中访寻，

一个娇好的少女见弃于情人；

倘见那薄幸的青年在她近前，

就把它轻轻地点上他的眼边。

他的身上穿着雅典人的装束，

你须仔细辨认清楚，不许弄错；

小心地执行着我谆谆的吩咐，

让他无限的柔情都向她倾吐。

等第一声雄鸡啼时我们再见。

迫克：　放心吧，主人，一切如你的意念。（各下。）

ACT II SCENE II

Another part of the wood.
[*Enter Titania, with her train.*]

TITANIA.   Come now, a roundel and a fairy song;
    Then, for the third part of a minute, hence:
    Some to kill cankers in the musk-rose buds;
    Some war with rere-mice for their leathern wings,
    To make my small elves coats; and some keep back
    The clamorous owl that nightly hoots and wonders
    At our quaint spirits. Sing me now asleep;
    Then to your offices, and let me rest.

[*The Fairies Sing.*]

FAIRY I.

You spotted snakes with double tongue,
Thorny hedgehogs, be not seen;
Newts and blind-worms, do no wrong,
Come not near our fairy Queen.
Philomel with melody
Sing in our sweet lullaby.
Lulla, lulla, lullaby;

第二幕　第二场

林中的另一处。

（提泰妮娅及其小仙侍从等上。）

提泰妮娅：　来，跳一回舞，唱一曲神仙歌，然后在一分钟内余下
　　来的三分之一的时间里，大家散开去；有的去杀死麝香玫瑰嫩
　　苞中的蛀虫；有的去和蝙蝠作战，剥下它们的翼革来为我的小
　　妖儿们做外衣；剩下的去驱逐每夜啼叫、看见我们这些伶俐的
　　小精灵们而惊骇的猫头鹰。现在唱歌给我催眠吧；唱罢之后，
　　大家各做各的事，让我休息一会儿。

（小仙们唱：）

一

两舌的花蛇，多刺的蝟，
　　不要打扰着她的安睡；
蝾螈和蜥蜴，不要行近，
　　仔细毒害了她的宁静。
夜莺，鼓起你的清弦，
　　为我们唱一曲催眠：
睡啦，睡啦，睡睡吧！

lulla, lulla, lullaby.

Never harm

Nor spell nor charm

Come our lovely lady nigh.

So good night, with lullaby.

FAIRY II.

Weaving spiders, come not here;

Hence, you long-legged spinners, hence.

Beetles black, approach not near;

Worm nor snail do no offence.

Philomel with melody, etc.

FAIRY I.　　Hence away; now all is well.

One aloof stand sentinel.

[*Exeunt Fairies. Titania sleeps.*]

[*Enter Oberon and squeezes the flower on Titania's eyelids.*]

OBERON.　　What thou seest when thou dost wake,

Do it for thy true-love take;

Love and languish for his sake.

Be it ounce, or cat, or bear,

Pard, or boar with bristled hair,

In thy eye that shall appear

When thou wak'st, it is thy dear.

　　　睡啦，睡啦，睡睡吧！

　　一切害物远走高飏，

　　　不要行近她的身旁；

　　　　晚安，睡睡吧！

二

　　织网的蜘蛛，不要过来；

　　　长脚的蛛儿快快走开！

　　黑背的蜣螂，不许走近；

　　不许莽撞，蜗牛和蚯蚓。

　　夜莺，鼓起你的清弦，

　　　为我们唱一曲催眠：

　　　睡啦，睡啦，睡睡吧！

　　　睡啦，睡啦，睡睡吧！

　　一切害物远走高飏，

　　　不要行近她的身旁；

　　　　晚安，睡睡吧！

一小仙：　去吧！现在一切都已完成，只需留着一个人作哨兵。

（众小仙下，提泰妮娅睡。）

（奥布朗上，挤花汁滴在提泰妮娅眼皮上。）

奥布朗：　等你眼睛一睁开，你就看见你的爱，为他担起相思债：

　　　山猫、豹子、大狗熊，野猪身上毛蓬蓬；等你醒来一看见丑东

　　　西在你身边，芳心可可为他恋。（下。）

Wake when some vile thing is near.

[*Exit.*]

[*Enter Lysander and Hermia.*]

LYSANDE.　Fair love, you faint with wandering in the wood;

　　　　And, to speak troth, I have forgot our way;

　　　　We'll rest us, Hermia, if you think it good,

　　　　And tarry for the comfort of the day.

HERMIA.　Be it so, Lysander: find you out a bed,

　　　　For I upon this bank will rest my head.

LYSANDE.　One turf shall serve as pillow for us both;

　　　　One heart, one bed, two bosoms, and one troth.

HERMIA.　Nay, good Lysander; for my sake, my dear,

　　　　Lie further off yet; do not lie so near.

LYSANDE.　O, take the sense, sweet, of my innocence!

　　　　Love takes the meaning in love's conference.

　　　　I mean that my heart unto yours is knit,

　　　　So that but one heart we can make of it;

　　　　Two bosoms interchained with an oath,

　　　　So then two bosoms and a single troth.

　　　　Then by your side no bed-room me deny,

　　　　For lying so, Hermia, I do not lie.

HERMIA.　Lysander riddles very prettily.

　　　　Now much beshrew my manners and my pride,

　　　　If Hermia meant to say Lysander lied!

（拉山德及赫米娅上。）

拉山德：　好人，你在林中东奔西走，疲乏得快要昏倒了。说老实话，我已经忘记了我们的路。要是你同意，赫米娅，让我们休息一下，等待到天亮再说。

赫米娅：　就照你的意思吧，拉山德。你去给你自己找一处睡眠的所在，因为我要在这花坛安息我的形骸。

拉山德：　一块草地可以作我们两人枕首的地方；两个胸膛一条心，应该合睡一个眠床。

赫米娅：　哎，不要，亲爱的拉山德；为着我的缘故，我的亲亲，再躺远一些，不要挨得那么近。

拉山德：　啊，爱人！不要误会了我的无邪的本意，恋人们原是能够领会彼此所说的话的。我是说我的心和你的心连结在一起，已经打成一片，分不开来；两个心胸彼此用盟誓连系，共有着一片忠贞。因此不要拒绝我睡在你的身旁，赫米娅，我一点没有坏心肠。

赫米娅：　拉山德真会说话。要是赫米娅疑心拉山德有坏心肠，愿她从此不能堂堂做人。但是好朋友，为着爱情和礼貌的缘故，请睡得远一些；在人间的礼法上，保持这样的距离对于束身自

But, gentle friend, for love and courtesy

Lie further off, in human modesty;

Such separation as may well be said

Becomes a virtuous bachelor and a maid,

So far be distant; and good night, sweet friend.

Thy love ne'er alter till thy sweet life end!

LYSANDE.　Amen, amen, to that fair prayer say I;

And then end life when I end loyalty!

Here is my bed; sleep give thee all his rest!

HERMIA.　With half that wish the wisher's eyes be pressed!

[*They sleep.*]

[*Enter Puck.*]

PUCK.　Through the forest have I gone,

But Athenian found I none

On whose eyes I might approve

This flower's force in stirring love.

Night and silence – Who is here?

Weeds of Athens he doth wear:

This is he, my master said,

Despised the Athenian maid;

And here the maiden, sleeping sound,

On the dank and dirty ground.

Pretty soul! she durst not lie

Near this lack-love, this kill-courtesy.

好的未婚男女，是最为合适的。这么远就行了。晚安，亲爱的
朋友！愿爱情永无更改，直到你生命的尽头！

拉山德： 依着你那祈祷我应和着阿门！阿门！我将失去我的生命，
　　　　 如其我失去我的忠贞！（略就远处退卧。）这里是我的眠床了；
　　　　 但愿睡眠给予你充分的休养！
赫米娅： 那愿望我愿意和你分享！
　　　　 （二人入睡。）

（迫克上。）

迫克： 我已经在森林中间走遍，
　　　 但雅典人可还不曾瞧见，
　　　 我要把这花液在他眼上
　　　 试一试激动爱情的力量。
　　　 静寂的深宵！啊，谁在这厢？
　　　 他身上穿着雅典的衣裳。
　　　 我那主人所说的正是他，
　　　 狠心地欺负那美貌娇娃；
　　　 她正在这一旁睡得酣熟，
　　　 不顾到地上的潮湿龌龊：
　　　 美丽的人儿！她竟然不敢
　　　 睡近这没有心肝的恶汉。

Churl, upon thy eyes I throw

[*Squeezes the flower on Lysander's eyelids.*]

All the power this charm doth owe:

When thou wak'st let love forbid

Sleep his seat on thy eyelid.

So awake when I am gone;

For I must now to Oberon.

[*Exit.*]

[*Enter Demetrius and Helena, running.*]

HELENA.   Stay, though thou kill me, sweet Demetrius.

DEMETR.   I charge thee, hence, and do not haunt me thus.

HELENA.   O, wilt thou darkling leave me? Do not so.

DEMETR.   Stay on thy peril; I alone will go.

   [*Exit.*]

HELENA.   O, I am out of breath in this fond chase!

   The more my prayer, the lesser is my grace.

   Happy is Hermia, wheresoe'er she lies,

   For she hath blessed and attractive eyes.

   How came her eyes so bright? Not with salt tears;

   If so, my eyes are oftener washed than hers.

   No, no, I am as ugly as a bear,

   For beasts that meet me run away for fear;

   Therefore no marvel though Demetrius

我已在你眼睛上，坏东西！

（挤花汁滴拉山德眼上。）

倾注着魔术的力量神奇；

等你醒来的时候，让爱情

从此扰乱你睡眠的安宁！

别了，你醒来我早已去远，

奥布朗在盼我和他见面。

（下。）

（狄米特律斯及海丽娜奔跑而上。）

海丽娜：　你杀死了我也好，但是请你停步吧，亲爱的狄米特律斯！

狄米特律斯：　我命令你走开，不要这样缠扰着我！

海丽娜：　啊！你要把我丢在黑暗中吗？请不要这样！

狄米特律斯：　站住！否则叫你活不成。我要独自走我的路。

（下。）

海丽娜：　唉！这痴心的追赶使我乏得透不过气来。我越是千求万
　　告，越是惹他憎恶。赫米娅无论在什么地方都是那么幸福，因
　　为她有一双天赐的迷人的眼睛。她的眼睛怎么会这样明亮呢？
　　不是为着泪水的缘故，因为我的眼睛被眼泪洗着的时候比她更
　　多。不，不，我是像一头熊那么难看，就是野兽看见我也会因
　　害怕而逃走；因此难怪狄米特律斯会这样逃避我，就像逃避一
　　个丑妖怪一样。哪一面欺人的坏镜子使我居然敢把自己跟赫米
　　娅的明星一样的眼睛相比呢？但是谁在这里？拉山德！躺在地
　　上！死了吗，还是睡了？我看不见有血，也没有伤处。拉山德，

Do, as a monster, fly my presence thus.

What wicked and dissembling glass of mine

Made me compare with Hermia's sphery eyne?

But who is here? Lysander! on the ground!

Dead, or asleep? I see no blood, no wound.

Lysander, if you live, good sir, awake.

LYSANDE.   [*Waking.*] And run through fire I will for thy sweet sake.

Transparent Helena! Nature shows art,

That through thy bosom makes me see thy heart.

Where is Demetrius? O, how fit a word

Is that vile name to perish on my sword!

HELENA.   Do not say so, Lysander; say not so.

What though he love your Hermia? Lord, what though?

Yet Hermia still loves you; then be content.

LYSANDE.   Content with Hermia! No: I do repent

The tedious minutes I with her have spent.

Not Hermia but Helena I love:

Who will not change a raven for a dove?

The will of man is by his reason swayed,

And reason says you are the worthier maid.

Things growing are not ripe until their season;

So I, being young, till now ripe not to reason;

And touching now the point of human skill,

Reason becomes the marshal to my will,

And leads me to your eyes, where I o'erlook

Love's stories, written in Love's richest book.

要是你没有死，好朋友，醒醒吧！

拉山德：　（醒。）我愿为着你赴汤蹈火，玲珑剔透的海丽娜！上天在你身上显出他的本领，使我能在你的胸前看透你的心。狄米特律斯在哪里？嘿！那个难听的名字让他死在我的剑下多么合适！

海丽娜：　不要这样说，拉山德！不要这样说！即使他爱你的赫米娅又有什么关系？上帝！那又有什么关系？赫米娅仍旧是爱着你的，所以你应该心满意足了。

拉山德：　跟赫米娅心满意足吗？不，我真悔恨和她在一起度着的那些可厌的时辰。我不爱赫米娅，我爱的是海丽娜；谁不愿意把一只乌鸦换一头白鸽呢？男人的意志是被理性所支配的，理性告诉我你比她更值得敬爱。凡是生长的东西，不到季节，总不会成熟：我过去由于年轻，我的理性也不曾成熟；但是现在我的智慧已经充分成长，理性指挥着我的意志，把我引到了你的眼前；在你的眼睛里我可以读到写在最丰美的爱情的经典上的故事。

HELENA.   Wherefore was I to this keen mockery born?

When at your hands did I deserve this scorn?

Is't not enough, is't not enough, young man,

That I did never, no, nor never can,

Deserve a sweet look from Demetrius' eye,

But you must flout my insufficiency?

Good troth, you do me wrong, good sooth, you do,

In such disdainful manner me to woo.

But fare you well; perforce I must confess

I thought you lord of more true gentleness.

O, that a lady of one man refused

Should of another therefore be abused!

[*Exit.*]

LYSANDE.   She sees not Hermia. Hermia, sleep thou there;

And never mayst thou come Lysander near!

For, as a surfeit of the sweetest things

The deepest loathing to the stomach brings,

Or as the heresies that men do leave

Are hated most of those they did deceive,

So thou, my surfeit and my heresy,

Of all be hated, but the most of me!

And, all my powers, address your love and might

To honour Helen, and to be her knight!

[*Exit.*]

HERMIA.   [*Starting.*] Help me, Lysander, help me; do thy best

海丽娜：　我怎么忍受得下这种尖刻的嘲笑呢？我什么时候得罪了你，使你这样讥讽我呢？我从来不曾得到过，也永远不会得到，狄米特律斯的一瞥爱怜的眼光，难道那还不够，难道那还不够，年轻人，你必须再这样挖苦我的短处吗？真的，你侮辱了我；真的，用这种卑鄙的样子向我献假殷勤。但是再会吧！我还以为你是个较有教养的上流人哩。唉！一个女子受到了这一个男人的摈拒，还得忍受那一个男子的揶揄。（下。）

拉山德：　她没有看见赫米娅。赫米娅，睡你的吧，再不要走近拉山德的身边了！一个人吃饱了太多的甜食，能使胸胃中发生强烈的厌恶，改信正教的人最是痛心疾首于以往欺骗他的异端邪说；你就是我的甜食和异端邪说，让你被一切的人所憎恶吧，但没有别人比我更憎恶你了。我的一切生命之力啊，用爱和力来尊崇海丽娜，做她的忠实的骑士吧！（下。）

赫米娅：　（醒。）救救我，拉山德！救救我！用出你全身力量来，

To pluck this crawling serpent from my breast.

Ay me, for pity! What a dream was here!

Lysander, look how I do quake with fear.

Methought a serpent eat my heart away,

And you sat smiling at his cruel prey.

Lysander! What, removed? Lysander! lord!

What, out of hearing gone? No sound, no word?

Alack, where are you? Speak, an if you hear;

Speak, of all loves! I swoon almost with fear.

No? Then I well perceive you are not nigh.

Either death or you I'll find immediately.

[*Exit.*]

替我在胸口上撵掉这条蠕动的蛇。哎呀，天哪！做了怎样的梦！拉山德，瞧我怎样因害怕而颤抖着。我觉得仿佛一条蛇在嚼食我的心，而你坐在一旁，瞧着它的残酷的肆虐微笑。拉山德！怎么！换了地方了？拉山德！好人！怎么！听不见？去了？没有声音，不说一句话？唉！你在哪儿？要是你听见我，答应一声呀！凭着一切爱情的名义，说话呀！我害怕得差不多要晕倒了。仍旧一声不响！我明白你已不在近旁了；要是我寻不到你，我定将一命丧亡！　（下。）

ACT III SCENE I

The wood. Titania lying asleep.

[*Enter Quince, Snug, Bottom, Flute, Snout, and Starveling.*]

BOTTOM.   Are we all met?

QUINCE.   Pat, pat; and here's a marvellous convenient place for our rehearsal. This green plot shall be our stage, this hawthorn brake our tiring-house; and we will do it in action, as we will do it before the Duke.

BOTTOM.   Peter Quince!

QUINCE.   What sayest thou, bully Bottom?

BOTTOM.   There are things in this comedy of Pyramus and Thisbe that will never please. First, Pyramus must draw a sword to kill himself; which the ladies cannot abide. How answer you that?

SNOUT.   By'r lakin, a parlous fear.

STARV.   I believe we must leave the killing out, when all is done.

BOTTOM.   Not a whit; I have a device to make all well. Write me a prologue; and let the prologue seem to say we will do no harm with our swords, and that Pyramus is not killed indeed; and for the more better assurance, tell them that I Pyramus am not Pyramus but Bottom the weaver. This will put them out of fear.

第三幕　第一场

林中。提泰妮娅熟睡未醒。

（昆斯、斯纳格、波顿、弗鲁特、斯诺特、斯塔佛林上。）

波顿：　咱们都会齐了吗？

昆斯：　妙极了，妙极了，这儿真是给咱们练戏用的一块再方便也
　　　　没有的地方。这块草地可以做咱们的戏台，这一丛山楂树便是
　　　　咱们的后台。咱们可以认真扮演一下；就像当着公爵殿下的面
　　　　前一样。

波顿：　彼得·昆斯，——

昆斯：　你说什么，波顿好家伙？

波顿：　在这本《皮拉摩斯和提斯柏》的喜剧里，有几个地方准难
　　　　叫人家满意。第一，皮拉摩斯该得拔出剑来结果自己的性命，
　　　　这是太太小姐们受不了的。你说可对不对？

斯诺特：　凭着圣母娘娘的名字，这可真的不是玩儿的事。

斯塔佛林：　我说咱们把什么都做完了之后，这一段自杀可不用表
　　　　演。

波顿：　不必，咱有一个好法子。给咱写一段开场诗，让这段开场
　　　　诗大概这么说：咱们的剑是不会伤人的；实实在在皮拉摩斯并
　　　　不真的把自己干掉了；顶好再那么声明一下，咱扮着皮拉摩斯
　　　　的，并不是皮拉摩斯，实在是织工波顿；这么一下她们就不会
　　　　受惊了。

QUINCE.　Well, we will have such a prologue; and it shall be written in eight and six.

BOTTOM.　No, make it two more; let it be written in eight and eight.

SNOUT.　Will not the ladies be afeard of the lion?

STARV.　I fear it, I promise you.

BOTTOM.　Masters, you ought to consider with yourselves: to bring in-God shield us! – a lion among ladies is a most dreadful thing; for there is not a more fearful wild-fowl than your lion living; and we ought to look to't.

SNOUT.　Therefore another prologue must tell he is not a lion.

BOTTOM.　Nay, you must name his name, and half his face must be seen through the lion's neck; and he himself must speak through, saying thus, or to the same defect: Ladies, or Fair ladies, I would wish you or I would request you or I would entreat you not to fear, not to tremble. My life for yours! If you think I come hither as a lion, it were pity of my life. No, I am no such thing; I am a man as other men are. And there, indeed, let him name his name, and tell them plainly he is Snug the joiner.

QUINCE.　Well, it shall be so. But there is two hard things ‐ that is, to bring the moonlight into a chamber; for, you know, Pyramus and Thisbe meet by moonlight.

SNOUT.　Doth the moon shine that night we play our play?

BOTTOM.　A calendar, a calendar! Look in the almanack; find out moonshine, find out moonshine.

QUINCE.　Yes, it doth shine that night.

BOTTOM.　Why, then may you leave a casement of the great

昆斯：　好吧，就让咱们有这么一段开场诗，咱可以把它写成八六体。

波顿：　把它再加上两个字，让它是八个字八个字那么的吧。

斯诺特：　太太小姐们见了狮子不会哆嗦吗？

斯塔佛林：　咱担保她们一定会害怕。

波顿：　列位，你们得好好想一想：把一头狮子——老天爷保佑咱们！——带到太太小姐们的中间，还有比这更荒唐得可怕的事吗？在野兽中间，狮子是再凶恶不过的。咱们可得考虑考虑。

斯诺特：　那么说，就得再写一段开场诗，说他并不是真狮子。

波顿：　不，你应当把他的名字说出来，他的脸蛋的一半要露在狮子头颈的外边；他自己就该说着这样或者诸如此类的话："太太小姐们，"或者说，"尊贵的太太小姐们，咱要求你们，"或者说，"咱请求你们，"或者说，"咱恳求你们，不用害怕，不用发抖；咱可以用生命给你们担保。要是你们想咱真是一头狮子，那咱才真是倒霉啦！不，咱完全不是这种东西；咱是跟别人一样的人。"这么着让他说出自己的名字来，明明白白地告诉她们，他是细工木匠斯纳格。

昆斯：　好吧，就这么办。但是还有两件难事：第一，咱们要把月亮光搬进屋子里来；你们知道皮拉摩斯和提斯柏是在月亮底下相见的。

斯纳格：　咱们演戏的那天可有月亮吗？

波顿：　拿历本来，拿历本来！瞧历本上有没有月亮，有没有月亮。

昆斯：　有的，那晚上有好月亮。

波顿：　啊，那么你就可以把咱们演戏的大厅上的一扇窗打开，月

chamber window, where we play, open; and the moon may shine in at the casement.

QUINCE.　Ay; or else one must come in with a bush of thorns and a lantern, and say he comes to disfigure or to present the person of Moonshine. Then there is another thing: we must have a wall in the great chamber; for Pyramus and Thisbe, says the story, did talk through the chink of a wall.

SNOUT.　You can never bring in a wall. What say you, Bottom?

BOTTOM.　Some man or other must present Wall; and let him have some plaster, or some loam, or some rough-cast about him, to signify wall; and let him hold his fingers thus, and through that cranny shall Pyramus and Thisbe whisper.

QUINCE.　If that may be, then all is well. Come, sit down, every mother's son, and rehearse your parts. Pyramus, you begin; when you have spoken your speech, enter into that brake; and so every one according to his cue.

[Enter Puck behind.]

PUCK.　What hempen homespuns have we swaggering here,So near the cradle of the Fairy Queen?

What, a play toward! I'll be an auditor;

An actor too perhaps, if I see cause.

QUINCE.　Speak, Pyramus. Thisbe, stand forth.

BOTTOM.　Thisbe, the flowers of odious savours sweet —

亮就会打窗子里照进来啦。

昆斯： 对了；否则就得叫一个人一手拿着柴枝，一手举起灯笼，登场说他是假扮或是代表着月亮。现在还有一件事，咱们在大厅里应该有一堵墙；因为故事上说，皮拉摩斯和提斯柏是彼此凑着一条墙缝讲话的。

斯纳格： 你可不能把一堵墙搬进来。你怎么说，波顿？

波顿： 让什么人扮作墙头；让他身上涂着些灰泥黏土之类，表明他是墙头；让他把手指举起作成那个样儿，皮拉摩斯和提斯柏就可以在手指缝里低声谈话了。

昆斯： 那样的话，一切就都已齐全了。来，每个老娘的儿子都坐下来，念着你们的台词。皮拉摩斯，你开头；你说完了之后，就走进那簇树后；这样大家可以按着尾白[1]挨次说下去。

（迫克自后上。）

迫克： 那一群伧夫俗子胆敢在仙后卧榻之旁鼓唇弄舌？哈，在那儿演戏！让我做一个听戏的吧；要是看到机会的话，也许我还要做一个演员哩。

昆斯： 说吧，皮拉摩斯。提斯柏，站出来。

波顿： 提斯柏，花儿开得十分香——

---

[1] 尾白指一句特定的台词。第一个演员念到"尾白"时，第二个演员便开始接话。

QUINCE.   Odious – odorous!

BOTTOM.   – dours savours sweet;

    So hath thy breath, my dearest Thisbe dear.

    But hark, a voice! Stay thou but here awhile,

    And by and by I will to thee appear.

    [*Exit.*]

PUCK.   A stranger Pyramus than e'er played here!

    [*Exit.*]

FLUTE.   Must I speak now?

QUINCE.   Ay, marry, must you; for you must understand he goes but
    to see a noise that he heard, and is to come again.

FLUTE.   Most radiant Pyramus, most lily-white of hue,

    Of colour like the red rose on triumphant brier,

    Most brisky juvenal, and eke most lovely Jew,

    As true as truest horse, that would never tire,

    I'll meet thee, Pyramus, at Ninny's tomb.

QUINCE.   Ninus' tomb, man! Why, you must not speak that yet; that
    you answer to Pyramus. You speak all your part at once, cues, and
    all. Pyramus enter: your cue is past; it is never tire.

FLUTE.   O – As true as truest horse, that yet would never tire.

[*Re-enter Puck, and Bottom with an ass's head.*]

BOTTOM.   If I were fair, Thisbe, I were only thine.

昆斯：　十分香，十分香。

波顿：　——开得十分香；你的气息，好人儿，也是一个样。听，
　　　　那边有一个声音，你且等一等，一会儿咱再来和你诉衷情。（下。）

迫克：　请看皮拉摩斯变成了怪妖精。（下。）

弗鲁特：　现在该咱说了吧？

昆斯：　是的，该你说。你得弄清楚，他是去瞧瞧什么声音去的，
　　　　等一会儿就要回来。

弗鲁特：　最俊美的皮拉摩斯，脸孔红如红玫瑰，
　　　　肌肤白得赛过纯白的百合花，
　　　　活泼的青年，最可爱的宝贝，
　　　　忠心耿耿像一匹顶好的马。
　　　　皮拉摩斯，咱们在宁尼的坟头相会。

昆斯：　"尼纳斯的坟头"，老兄。你不要就把这句说出来，那是
　　　　要你答应皮拉摩斯的；你把要你说的话不管什么尾白不尾白都
　　　　一股脑儿说出来啦。皮拉摩斯，进来；你的尾白已经说过了，
　　　　是"顶好的马"。

弗鲁特：　噢。——忠心耿耿像一匹顶好的马。

（迫克重上；波顿戴驴头随上。）

波顿：　美丽的提斯柏，咱是整个儿属于你的！

QUINCE.　O monstrous! O strange! We are haunted. Pray, masters! fly, masters! Help!

[*Exeunt all but Bottom and Puck.*]

PUCK.　I'll follow you; I'll lead you about a round,

Through bog, through bush, through brake, through brier;

Sometime a horse I'll be, sometime a hound,

A hog, a headless bear, sometime a fire;

And neigh, and bark, and grunt, and roar, and burn,

Like horse, hound, hog, bear, fire, at every turn.

[*Exit.*]

BOTTOM.　Why do they run away? This is a knavery of them to make me afeard.

[*Re-enter Snout.*]

SNOUT.　O Bottom, thou art changed! What do I see on thee?

BOTTOM.　What do you see? You see an ass-head of your own, do you?

[*Exit Snout.*]

[*Re-enter Quince.*]

QUINCE.　Bless thee, Bottom, bless thee! Thou art translated.

[*Exit.*]

昆斯：　怪事！怪事！咱们见了鬼啦！列位，快逃！快逃！救命哪！

（众下。）

迫克：　我要把你们带领得团团乱转，

　　　　经过一处处沼地、草莽和林薮；

　　　　有时我化作马，有时化作猎犬，

　　　　化作野猪、没头的熊或是燐火；

　　　　我要学马样嘶，犬样吠，猪样噑，

　　　　熊一样的咆哮，野火一样燃烧。

　　　　（下。）

波顿：　他们干么都跑走了呢？这准是他们的恶计，要把咱吓一跳。

（斯诺特重上。）

斯诺特：　啊，波顿！你变了样子啦！你头上是什么东西呀？

波顿：　是什么东西？你瞧见你自己变成了一头蠢驴啦，是不是？

　　　　（斯诺特下。）

（昆斯重上。）

昆斯：　天哪！波顿！天哪！你变啦！（下。）

BOTTOM. I see their knavery: this is to make an ass of me; to fright me, if they could. But I will not stir from this place, do what they can; I will walk up and down here, and will sing, that they shall hear I am not afraid. [*Sings.*]

The ousel cock, so black of hue,

With orange-tawny bill,

The throstle with his note so true,

The wren with little quill.

TITANIA. [*Awaking.*] What angel wakes me from my flowery bed?

BOTTOM. [*Sings.*] The finch, the sparrow, and the lark,

The plain-song cuckoo grey,

Whose note full many a man doth mark,

And dares not answer nay – for, indeed, who would set his wit to so foolish a bird?Who would give a bird the lie, though he cry cuckoo never so?

TITANIA. I pray thee, gentle mortal, sing again.

Mine ear is much enamoured of thy note;

So is mine eye enthralled to thy shape;

And thy fair virtue's force perforce doth move me,

On the first view, to say, to swear, I love thee.

BOTTOM. Methinks, mistress, you should have little reason for that. And yet, to say the truth, reason and love keep little company together now-a-days. The more the pity that some honest neighbours will not make them friends. Nay, I can gleek upon occasion.

TITANIA. Thou art as wise as thou art beautiful.

波顿：　咱看透他们的鬼把戏；他们要把咱当做一头蠢驴，想出法子来吓咱。可是咱决不离开这块地方，瞧他们怎么办。咱要在这儿跑来跑去；咱要唱个歌儿，让他们听见了知道咱可一点不怕。（唱）

> 山乌嘴巴黄沉沉，
>
> 浑身长满黑羽毛，
>
> 画眉唱得顶认真，
>
> 声音尖细是欧鹟。

提泰妮娅：　（醒。）什么天使使我从百花的卧榻上醒来呢？

波顿：　（唱）

> 鹡鸰，麻雀，百灵鸟，
>
> 还有杜鹃爱骂人，
>
> 大家听了心头恼，
>
> 可是谁也不回声。

真的，谁耐烦跟这么一头蠢鸟斗口舌呢？即使它骂你是乌龟，谁又高兴跟他争辩呢？

提泰妮娅：　温柔的凡人，请你唱下去吧！我的耳朵沉醉在你的歌声里，我的眼睛又为你的状貌所迷惑；在第一次见面的时候，你的美姿已使我不禁说出而且矢誓着我爱你了。

波顿：　咱想，奶奶，您这可太没有理由。不过说老实话，现今世界上理性可真难得跟爱情碰头；也没有哪位正直的邻居大叔给他俩撮合撮合做朋友，真是抱歉得很。哈，我有时也会说说笑话。

提泰妮娅：　你真是又聪明又美丽。

BOTTOM.　Not so, neither; but if I had wit enough to get out of this wood, I have enough to serve mine own turn.

TITANIA.　Out of this wood do not desire to go;

Thou shalt remain here whether thou wilt or no.

I am a spirit of no common rate;

The summer still doth tend upon my state;

And I do love thee; therefore, go with me.

I'll give thee fairies to attend on thee;

And they shall fetch thee jewels from the deep,

And sing, while thou on pressed flowers dost sleep;

And I will purge thy mortal grossness so

That thou shalt like an airy spirit go.

Peasblossom! Cobweb! Moth! and Mustardseed!

[*Enter Peasblossom, Cobweb, Moth, and Mustardseed.*]

PEASE.　Ready.

COBWEB.　And I.

MOTH.　And I.

MUSTARD.　And I.

ALL FOUR.　Where shall we go?

TITANIA.　Be kind and courteous to this gentleman;

Hop in his walks and gambol in his eyes;

Feed him with apricocks and dewberries,

With purple grapes, green figs, and mulberries;

The honey bags steal from the humble-bees,

波顿：　　不见得，不见得。可是咱要是有本事跑出这座林子，那已经很够了。

提泰妮娅：　请不要跑出这座林子！不论你愿不愿，你一定要留在这里。我不是一个平常的精灵，夏天永远听从我的命令；我真是爱你，因此跟我去吧。我将使神仙们侍候你，他们会从海底里捞起珍宝献给你；当你在花茵上睡去的时候，他们会给你歌唱；而且我要给你洗涤去俗体的污垢，使你身轻得像个精灵一样。豆花！蛛网！飞蛾！芥子！

（四神仙上。）

豆花：　　有。

蛛网：　　有。

飞蛾：　　有。

芥子：　　有。

四仙：　　差我们到什么地方去？

提泰妮娅：　恭恭敬敬地侍候这先生，

　　　　　窜窜跳跳地追随他前行；

　　　　　给他吃杏子、鹅莓和桑葚，

　　　　　紫葡萄和无花果儿青青。

　　　　　去把野蜂的蜜囊儿偷取，

And for night-tapers crop their waxen thighs,

And light them at the fiery glow-worm's eyes,

To have my love to bed and to arise;

And pluck the wings from painted butterflies,

To fan the moonbeams from his sleeping eyes.

Nod to him, elves, and do him courtesies.

PEASE.　Hail, mortal!

COBWEB.　Hail!

MOTH.　Hail!

MUSTARD.　Hail!

BOTTOM.　I cry your worships mercy, heartily; I beseech your worship's name.

COBWEB.　Cobweb.

BOTTOM.　I shall desire you of more acquaintance, good Master Cobweb. If I cut my finger, I shall make bold with you. Your name, honest gentleman?

PEASE.　Peasblossom.

BOTTOM.　I pray you, commend me to Mistress Squash, your mother, and to Master Peascod, your father. Good Master Peasblossom, I shall desire you of more acquaintance you're your name, I beseech you, sir?

MUSTAR.　Mustardseed.

BOTTOM.　Good Master Mustardseed, I know your patience well. That same cowardly giant-like ox-beef hath devoured many a gentleman of your house. I promise you your kindred hath made my eyes water ere now. I desire you of more acquaintance, good

剪下蜂股的蜂蜡做烛炬，
在流萤的火睛里点了火，
照着我的爱人晨兴夜卧；
再摘下彩蝶儿粉翼娇红，
搌去他眼上的月光溶溶。
来，向他鞠一个深深的躬。

豆花：　万福，凡人！

蛛网：　万福！

飞蛾：　万福！

芥子：　万福！

波顿：　请你们列位先生多多担待担待在下。请教大号是——？

蛛网：　蛛网。

波顿：　很希望跟您交个朋友，好蛛网先生；要是咱指头儿割破了
　　　　的话，咱要大胆用用您[1]。善良的先生，您的尊号是——？

豆花：　豆花。

波顿：　啊，请多多给咱向您令堂豆荚奶奶和令尊豆壳先生致意。好
　　　　豆花先生，咱也很希望跟您交个朋友。先生，您的雅号是——？

芥子：　芥子。

波顿：　好芥子先生，咱知道您是个饱历艰辛的人；那块庞大无比
　　　　的牛肉曾经把您家里好多人都吞去了。不瞒您说，您的亲戚们
　　　　方才还害得我掉下几滴苦泪呢。咱希望跟您交个朋友，好芥子

---

[1] 古代希腊人用蜘蛛丝止血。

Master Mustardseed.

TITANIA.　　Come, wait upon him; lead him to my bower.

　　The moon, methinks, looks with a watery eye;

　　And when she weeps, weeps every little flower;

　　Lamenting some enforced chastity.

　　Tie up my love's tongue, bring him silently.

　　[*Exeunt.*]

先生。

提泰妮娅：　　来，侍候着他，引路到我的闺房。

　　　　月亮今夜有一颗多泪的眼睛；

　　　　小花们也都陪着她眼泪汪汪，

　　　　悲悼横遭强暴而失去的童贞。

　　　　吩咐那好人静静走不许作声。

　　　　（同下。）

ACT III   SCENE II

Another part of the wood.
[*Enter Oberon.*]

OBERON.   I wonder if Titania be awaked;
　　　Then, what it was that next came in her eye,
　　　Which she must dote on in extremity.

[*Enter Puck.*]

OBERON.   Here comes my messenger. How now, mad spirit!
　　　What night-rule now about this haunted grove?
PUCK.　My mistress with a monster is in love.
　　　Near to her close and consecrated bower,
　　　While she was in her dull and sleeping hour,
　　　A crew of patches, rude mechanicals,
　　　That work for bread upon Athenian stalls,
　　　Were met together to rehearse a play
　　　Intended for great Theseus' nuptial day.
　　　The shallowest thickskin of that barren sort,
　　　Who Pyramus presented, in their sport
　　　Forsook his scene and ent'red in a brake;

第三幕　第二场

林中的另一处。
（奥布朗上。）

奥布朗：　不知道提泰妮娅有没有醒来；她一醒来，就要热烈地爱
　　上了她第一眼看到的无论什么东西了。这边来的是我的使者。

（迫克上。）

奥布朗：　啊，疯狂的精灵！在这座夜的魔林里现在有什么事情发
　　生？

迫克：　姑娘爱上了一个怪物了。当她昏昏睡熟的时候，在她的隐
　　秘的神圣的卧室之旁，来了一群村汉；他们都是在雅典市集上
　　做工过活的粗鲁的手艺人，聚集在一起练着戏，预备在忒修斯
　　结婚的那天表演。在这一群蠢货的中间，一个最蠢的蠢材扮演
　　着皮拉摩斯；当他退场走进一簇丛林里去的时候，我就抓住了
　　这个好机会，给他的头上罩上一只死驴的头壳。一会儿为了答
　　应他的提斯柏，这位好伶人又出来了。他们一看见了他，就像
　　雁子望见了蹑足行近的猎人，又像一大群灰鸦听见了枪声轰然
　　飞起乱叫、四散着横扫过天空一样，大家没命逃走了；又因为
　　我们的跳舞震动了地面，一个个横仆竖倒，嘴里乱喊着救命。

When I did him at this advantage take,

An ass's nowl I fixed on his head.

Anon his Thisbe must be answered,

And forth my mimic comes. When they him spy,

As wild geese that the creeping fowler eye,

Or russet-pated choughs, many in sort,

Rising and cawing at the gun's report,

Sever themselves and madly sweep the sky,

So at his sight away his fellows fly;

And at our stamp here, o'er and o'er one falls;

He murder cries, and help from Athens calls.

Their sense thus weak, lost with their fears thus strong,

Made senseless things begin to do them wrong,

For briers and thorns at their apparel snatch;

Some sleeves, some hats, from yielders all things catch.

I led them on in this distracted fear,

And left sweet Pyramus translated there;

When in that moment, so it came to pass,

Titania waked, and straightway loved an ass.

OBERON.   This falls out better than I could devise.

But hast thou yet latched the Athenian's eyes

With the love-juice, as I did bid thee do?

PUCK.   I took him sleeping – that is finished too –

And the Athenian woman by his side;

That, when he waked, of force she must be eyed.

[*Enter Demetrius and Hermia.*]

他们本来就是那么糊涂，这回吓得完全丧失了神智，没有知觉的东西也都来欺侮他们了：野茨和荆棘抓破了他们的衣服；有的失去了袖子，有的落掉了帽子，败军之将，无论什么东西都是予取予求的。在这种惊惶中我领着他们走去，把变了样子的可爱的皮拉摩斯孤单单地留下；就在那时候，提泰妮娅醒了转来，立刻爱上了一头驴子了。

奥布朗：　这比我所能想得到的计策还好。但是你有没有依照我的吩咐，把那爱汁滴在那个雅典人的眼上呢？

迫克：　那我也已经乘他睡熟的时候办好了。那个雅典女人就在他的身边，因此他一醒来，一定便会看见她。

（狄米特律斯及赫米娅上。）

OBERON.　Stand close; this is the same Athenian.

PUCK.　This is the woman, but not this the man.

DEMETR.　O, why rebuke you him that loves you so?

　　Lay breath so bitter on your bitter foe.

HERMIA.　Now I but chide, but I should use thee worse,

　　For thou, I fear, hast given me cause to curse.

　　If thou hast slain Lysander in his sleep,

　　Being o'er shoes in blood, plunge in the deep,

　　And kill me too.

　　The sun was not so true unto the day

　　As he to me. Would he have stolen away

　　From sleeping Hermia? I'll believe as soon

　　This whole earth may be bored, and that the moon

　　May through the centre creep and so displease

　　Her brother's noontide with the Antipodes.

　　It cannot be but thou hast murdered him;

　　So should a murderer look – so dead, so grim.

DEMETR.　So should the murdered look; and so should I,

　　Pierced through the heart with your stern cruelty;

　　Yet you, the murderer, look as bright, as clear,

　　As yonder Venus in her glimmering sphere.

HERMIA.　What's this to my Lysander? Where is he?

　　Ah, good Demetrius, wilt thou give him me?

DEMETR.　I had rather give his carcass to my hounds.

HERMIA.　Out, dog! out, cur! Thou driv'st me past the bounds

　　Of maiden's patience. Hast thou slain him, then?

奥布朗：　站过来些，这就是那个雅典人。

迫克：　这女人一点不错；那男人可不是。

狄米特律斯：　唉！为什么你这样骂着深爱你的人呢？那种毒骂是应该加在你仇敌身上的。

赫米娅：　现在我不过把你数说数说罢了；我应该更厉害地对付你，因为我相信你是可诅咒的。要是你已经乘着拉山德睡着的时候把他杀了，那么把我也杀了吧；已经两脚踏在血泊中，索性让杀人的血淹没你的膝盖吧。太阳对于白昼，也没有像他对于我那样的忠心。当赫米娅睡熟的时候，他会悄悄地离开她吗？我宁愿相信地球的中心可以穿成孔道，月亮会从里面钻了过去，在地球的那一端跟她的兄长白昼捣乱。一定是你已经把他杀死了；因为只有杀人的凶徒，脸上才会这样惨白而可怖。

狄米特律斯：　被杀者的脸色应该是这样的，你的残酷已经洞穿我的心，因此我应该有那样的脸色；但是你这杀人的，瞧上去却仍然是那么辉煌莹洁，就像那边天上闪耀着的金星一样。

赫米娅：　你这种话跟我的拉山德有什么关系？他在哪里呀？啊，好狄米特律斯，把他还给了我吧！

狄米特律斯：　我宁愿把他的尸体喂我的猎犬。

赫米娅：　滚开，贱狗！滚开，恶狗！你使我失去姑娘家的柔顺，再也忍不住了。你真的把他杀了吗？从此之后，别再把你算作

Henceforth be never numbered among men!

O, once tell true; tell true, even for my sake!

Durst thou have looked upon him being awake,

And hast thou killed him sleeping? O brave touch!

Could not a worm, an adder, do so much?

An adder did it; for with doubler tongue

Than thine, thou serpent, never adder stung.

DEMETR.   You spend your passion on a misprised mood:

I am not guilty of Lysander's blood;

Nor is he dead, for aught that I can tell.

HERMIA.   I pray thee, tell me then that he is well.

DEMETR.   An if I could, what should I get therefore?

HERMIA.   A privilege never to see me more.

And from thy hated presence part I so;

See me no more whether he be dead or no.

[*Exit.*]

DEMETR.   There is no following her in this fierce vein;

Here, therefore, for a while I will remain.

So sorrow's heaviness doth heavier grow

For debt that bankrupt sleep doth sorrow owe;

Which now in some slight measure it will pay,

If for his tender here I make some stay.

[*Lies down.*]

OBERON.   What hast thou done? Thou hast mistaken quite,

And laid the love-juice on some true-love's sight. Of thy

人吧！啊，看在我的面上，老老实实告诉我，告诉我，你，一个清醒的人，看见他睡着，而把他杀了吗？哎哟，真勇敢！一条蛇、一条毒蛇，都比不上你；因为它的分叉的毒舌，还不及你的毒心更毒！

狄米特律斯：　你的脾气发得好没来由。我并没有杀死拉山德，他也并没有死，照我所知道的。

赫米娅：　那么请你告诉我他很安全。

狄米特律斯：　要是我告诉你，我将得到什么好处呢？

赫米娅：　你可以得到永远不再看见我的权利。我从此离开你那可憎的脸；无论他死也罢活也罢，你再不要和我相见。（下。）

狄米特律斯：　在她这样盛怒之中，我还是不要跟着她。让我在这儿暂时停留一会儿。

睡眠欠下了沉忧的债，

心头加重了沉忧的担；

我且把黑甜乡暂时寻访，

还了些还不尽的糊涂账。

（卧下睡去。）

奥布朗：　你干了些什么事呢？你已经大大地弄错了，把爱汁去滴在一个真心的恋人的眼上。为了这次错误，本来忠实的将要改

misprision must perforce ensue

Some true love turned, and not a false turned true.

PUCK.　Then fate o'er-rules, that, one man holding troth,

A million fail, confounding oath on oath.

OBERON.　About the wood go swifter than the wind,

And Helena of Athens look thou find;

All fancy-sick she is and pale of cheer,

With sighs of love that costs the fresh blood dear.

By some illusion see thou bring her here;

I'll charm his eyes against she do appear.

PUCK.　I go, I go; look how I go,

Swifter than arrow from the Tartar's bow.

[*Exit.*]

OBERON.　Flower of this purple dye,

Hit with Cupid's archery,

Sink in apple of his eye.

When his love he doth espy,

Let her shine as gloriously

As the Venus of the sky.

When thou wak'st, if she be by,

Beg of her for remedy.

[*Re-enter Puck.*]

PUCK.　Captain of our fairy band,

变心肠，而不忠实的仍旧和以前一样。

迫克： 一切都是命运在做主；保持着忠心的不过一个人；变心的，
把盟誓起了一个毁了一个的，却有百万个人。

奥布朗： 比风还快地到林中各处去访寻名叫海丽娜的雅典女郎吧。
她是全然为爱情而憔悴的，痴心的叹息耗去了她脸上的血色。
用一些幻象把她引到这儿来：我将在这个人的眼睛上施上魔法，
准备他们的见面。

迫克： 我去，我去，瞧我一会儿便失了踪迹；鞑靼人的飞箭都赶
不上我的迅疾。（下。）

奥布朗： 这一朵紫色的小花，
尚留着爱神的箭疤，
让它那灵液的力量，
渗进他眸子的中央。
当他看见她的时光，
让她显出庄严妙相，
如同金星照亮天庭，
让他向她婉转求情。

（迫克重上。）

迫克： 报告神仙界的头脑，

Helena is here at hand,

And the youth mistook by me

Pleading for a lover's fee;

Shall we their fond pageant see?

Lord, what fools these mortals be!

OBERON.　Stand aside. The noise they make

Will cause Demetrius to awake.

PUCK.　Then will two at once woo one.

That must needs be sport alone;

And those things do best please me

That befall preposterously.

[*Enter Lysander and Helena.*]

LYSANDE.　Why should you think that I should woo in scorn?

Scorn and derision never come in tears.

Look when I vow, I weep; and vows so born,

In their nativity all truth appears.

How can these things in me seem scorn to you,

Bearing the badge of faith, to prove them true?

HELENA.　You do advance your cunning more and more.

When truth kills truth, O devilish-holy fray!

These vows are Hermia's. Will you give her o'er?

Weigh oath with oath, and you will nothing weigh:

Your vows to her and me, put in two scales,

Will even weigh; and both as light as tales.

海丽娜已被我带到，

她后面随着那少年，

正在哀求着她眷怜。

瞧瞧那痴愚的形状，

人们真蠢得没法想！

奥布朗：　站开些；他们的声音

　　　　将要惊醒睡着的人。

迫克：　两男合爱着一女，

　　　　这把戏真够有趣；

　　　　最妙是颠颠倒倒，

　　　　看着才叫人发笑。

（拉山德及海丽娜上。）

拉山德：　为什么你要以为我的求爱不过是向你嘲笑呢？嘲笑和戏
　　　　谑是永不会伴着眼泪而来的；瞧，我在起誓的时候是怎样感泣
　　　　着！这样的誓言是不会被人认作虚诳的。明明有着可以证明是
　　　　千真万确的表记，为什么你会以为我这一切都是出于姗笑呢？

海丽娜：　你越来越俏皮了。要是人们所说的真话都是互相矛盾的，
　　　　那么神圣的真话将成了一篇鬼话。这些誓言都是应当向赫米娅
　　　　说的；难道你把她丢弃了吗？把你对她和对我的誓言放在两个
　　　　秤盘里，一定称不出轻重来，因为都是像空话那样虚浮。

LYSANDE.   I hod no judgment when to her I swore.

HELENA.   Nor none, in my mind, now you give her o'er.

LYSANDE.   Demetrius loves her, and he loves not you.

DEMETR.   [*Awaking.*] O Helen, goddess, nymph, perfect, divine!

To what, my love, shall I compare thine eyne?

Crystal is muddy. O, how ripe in show

Thy lips, those kissing cherries, tempting grow!

That pure congealed white, high Taurus' snow,

Fanned with the eastern wind, turns to a crow

When thou hold'st up thy hand. O, let me kiss

This princess of pure white, this seal of bliss!

HELENA.   O spite! O hell! I see you all are bent

To set against me for your merriment.

If you were civil and knew courtesy,

You would not do me thus much injury.

Can you not hate me, as I know you do,

But you must join in souls to mock me too?

If you were men, as men you are in show,

You would not use a gentle lady so:

To vow, and swear, and superpraise my parts,

When I am sure you hate me with your hearts.

You both are rivals, and love Hermia;

And now both rivals, to mock Helena.

A trim exploit, a manly enterprise,

To conjure tears up in a poor maid's eyes

With your derision! None of noble sort

拉山德：　当我向她起誓的时候，我实在一点见识都没有。

海丽娜：　照我想起来，你现在把她丢弃了，也不像是有见识的。

拉山德：　狄米特律斯爱着她，但他不爱你。

狄米特律斯：　（醒。）啊，海伦[1]！完美的女神！圣洁的仙子！我要用什么来比并你的秀眼呢，我的爱人？水晶是太昏暗了。啊，你的嘴唇，那吻人的樱桃，瞧上去是多么成熟，多么诱人！你一举起你那洁白的妙手，被东风吹着的陶洛斯高山上的积雪，就显得像乌鸦那么黯黑了。让我吻一吻那纯白的女王，这幸福的象征吧！

海丽娜：　唉，倒霉！该死！我明白你们都在拿我取笑；假如你们是懂得礼貌和有教养的人，一定不会这样侮辱我。我知道你们都讨厌着我，那么就讨厌我好了，为什么还要联合起来讥讽我呢？你们瞧上去都像堂堂男子，如果真是堂堂男子，就不该这样对待一个有身份的妇女：发着誓，赌着咒，过誉着我的好处，但我可以断定你们的心里却在讨厌我。你们两人是情敌，一同爱着赫米娅，现在转过身来一同把海丽娜嘲笑，真是大丈夫的行为，干得真漂亮，为着取笑的缘故逼一个可怜的女人流泪！高尚的人绝不会这样轻侮一个闺女，逼到她忍无可忍，只是因为给你们寻寻开心。

---

[1] 海伦是海丽娜的爱称。

Would so offend a virgin, and extort

A poor soul's patience, all to make you sport.

LYSANDE.　You are unkind, Demetrius; be not so;

For you love Hermia. This you know I know;

And here, with all good will, with all my heart,

In Hermia's love I yield you up my part;

And yours of Helena to me bequeath,

Whom I do love and will do till my death.

HELENA.　Never did mockers waste more idle breath.

DEMETR.　Lysander, keep thy Hermia; I will none.

If e'er I loved her, all that love is gone.

My heart to her but as guest-wise sojourned,

And now to Helen is it home returned,

There to remain.

LYSANDE.　Helen, it is not so.

DEMETR.　Disparage not the faith thou dost not know,

Lest, to thy peril, thou aby it dear.

Look where thy love comes; yonder is thy dear.

[*Enter Hermia.*]

HERMIA.　Dark night, that from the eye his function takes,

The ear more quick of apprehension makes;

Wherein it doth impair the seeing sense,

It pays the hearing double recompense.

Thou art not by mine eye, Lysander, found;

拉山德： 你太残忍，狄米特律斯，不要这样；因为你爱着赫米娅，
　　　　 这你知道我是十分明白的。现在我用全心和好意把我在赫米娅
　　　　 的爱情中的地位让给你；但你也得把海丽娜的爱情让给我，因
　　　　 为我爱她，并且将要爱她到死。

海丽娜： 从来不曾有过嘲笑者浪费过这样无聊的口舌。

狄米特律斯： 拉山德，保留着你的赫米娅吧，我不要；要是我曾
　　　　 经爱过她，那爱情现在也已经消失了。我的爱不过像过客一样
　　　　 暂时驻留在她的身上，现在它已经回到它的永远的家，海丽娜
　　　　 的身边，再不到别处去了。

拉山德： 海伦，他的话是假的。

狄米特律斯： 不要侮蔑你所不知道的真理，否则你将以生命的危
　　　　 险重重补偿你的过失。瞧！你的爱人来了；那边才是你的爱人。

（赫米娅上。）

赫米娅： 黑夜使眼睛失去它的作用，但却使耳朵的听觉更为灵敏；
　　　　 它虽然妨碍了视觉的活动，却给予听觉加倍的补偿。我的眼睛
　　　　 不能寻到你，拉山德；但多谢我的耳朵，使我能听见你的声音。
　　　　 你为什么那样忍心地离开了我呢？

Mine ear, I thank it, brought me to thy sound.

But why unkindly didst thou leave me so?

LYSANDE.   Why should he stay whom love doth press to go?

HERMIA.   What love could press Lysander from my side?

LYSANDE.   Lysander's love, that would not let him bide –

Fair Helena, who more engilds the night

Than all yon fiery oes and eyes of light.

Why seek'st thou me? Could not this make thee know

The hate I bare thee made me leave thee so?

HERMIA.   You speak not as you think; it cannot be

HELENA.   Lo, she is one of this confederacy!

Now I perceive they have conjoined all three

To fashion this false sport in spite of me.Injurious Hermia! most ungrateful maid!

Have you conspired, have you with these contrived,

To bait me with this foul derision?

Is all the counsel that we two have shared,

The sisters' vows, the hours that we have spent,

When we have chid the hasty-footed time

For parting us – O, is all forgot?

All school-days' friendship, childhood innocence?

We, Hermia, like two artificial gods,

Have with our needles created both one flower,

Both on one sampler, sitting on one cushion,

Both warbling of one song, both in one key;

As if our hands, our sides, voices, and minds,

拉山德：　爱情驱着一个人走的时候，为什么他要滞留呢？

赫米娅：　哪一种爱情能把拉山德驱开我的身边？

拉山德：　拉山德的爱情使他一刻也不能停留；美丽的海丽娜，她
　　　　　照耀着夜天，使一切明亮的繁星黯然无色。为什么你要来寻找
　　　　　我呢？难道这还不能使你知道我因为厌恶你的缘故，才这样离
　　　　　开你吗？

赫米娅：　你说的不是真话；那不会是真的。

海丽娜：　瞧！她也是他们的一党。现在我明白了他们三个人一起
　　　　　联合了用这种恶戏欺凌我。欺人的赫米娅！最没有良心的丫头！
　　　　　你竟然和这种人一同算计着向我开这种卑鄙的玩笑作弄我吗？
　　　　　我们两人从前的种种推心置腹，约为姊妹的盟誓，在一起怨恨
　　　　　疾足的时间这样快便把我们拆分的那种时光，啊！你难道都已
　　　　　经忘记了吗？我们在同学时的那种情谊，一切童年的天真，你
　　　　　都已经完全丢在脑后了吗？赫米娅，我们两人曾经像两个巧手
　　　　　的神匠，在一起绣着同一朵花，描着同一个图样，我们同坐在
　　　　　一个椅垫上，齐声曼吟着同一个歌儿，就像我们的手、我们的
　　　　　身体、我们的声音、我们的思想，都是连在一起不可分的样子。
　　　　　我们这样生长在一起，正如并蒂的樱桃，看似两个，其实却连
　　　　　生在一起；我们是结在同一茎上的两颗可爱的果实，我们的身
　　　　　体虽然分开，我们的心却只有一个——原来我们的身子好比两
　　　　　个互通婚姻的名门，我们的心好比男家女家的纹章合而为一。
　　　　　难道你竟把我们从前的友好丢弃不顾，而和男人们联合着嘲弄
　　　　　你的可怜的朋友吗？这种行为太没有朋友的情谊，而且也不

Had been incorporate. So we grew together,

Like to a double cherry, seeming parted,

But yet an union in partition, ·

Two lovely berries moulded on one stern;

So, with two seeming bodies, but one heart;

Two of the first, like coats in heraldry,

Due but to one, and crowned with one crest.

And will you rent our ancient love asunder,

To join with men in scorning your poor friend?

It is not friendly, 'tis not maidenly;

Our sex, as well as I, may chide you for it,

Though I alone do feel the injury.

HERMIA.　I am amazed at your passionate words;

I scorn you not; it seems that you scorn me.

HELENA.　Have you not set Lysander, as in scorn,

To follow me and praise my eyes and face?

And made your other love, Demetrius,

Who even but now did spurn me with his foot,

To call me goddess, nymph, divine, and rare,

Precious, celestial? Wherefore speaks he this

To her he hates? And wherefore doth Lysander

Deny your love, so rich within his soul,

And tender me, forsooth, affection,

But by your setting on, by your consent?

What though I be not so in grace as you,

So hung upon with love, so fortunate,

合一个少女的身份。不单是我，我们全体女人都可以攻击你，
虽然受到委屈的只是我一个。

赫米娅：　你这种愤激的话真使我惊奇。我并没有嘲弄你；似乎你
　　　　在嘲弄我哩。

海丽娜：　你不曾唆使拉山德跟随我，假意称赞我的眼睛和面孔吗？
　　　　你那另一个爱人，狄米特律斯，不久之前还曾要用他的脚踢开
　　　　我，你不曾使他称我为女神、仙子，神圣而稀有的、珍贵的、
　　　　超乎一切的人吗？为什么他要向他所讨厌的人说这种话呢？
　　　　拉山德的灵魂里是充满了你的爱的，为什么他反而要摈斥你，
　　　　却要把他的热情奉献给我，倘不是因为你的指使，因为你们曾
　　　　经预先商量好？即使我不像你那样有人爱怜，那样被人追求不
　　　　舍，那样走好运，即使我是那样倒霉，得不到我所爱的人的爱
　　　　情，那和你又有什么关系呢？你应该可怜我才是，不应该反而
　　　　来侮蔑我。

But miserable most, to love unloved?

This you should pity rather than despise.

HERMIA.　I understand not what you mean by this.

HELENA.　Ay, do – persever, counterfeit sad looks,

Make mouths upon me when I turn my back,

Wink each at other; hold the sweet jest up;

This sport, well carried, shall be chronicled.

If you have any pity, grace, or manners,

You would not make me such an argument.

But fare ye well; 'tis partly my own fault,

Which death, or absence, soon shall remedy.

LYSANDE.　Stay, gentle Helena; hear my excuse;

My love, my life, my soul, fair Helena!

HELENA.　O excellent!

HERMIA.　Sweet, do not scorn her so.

DEMETR.　If she cannot entreat, I can compel.

LYSANDE.　Thou canst compel no more than she entreat;

Thy threats have no more strength than her weak prayers

Helen, I love thee, by my life I do;

I swear by that which I will lose for thee

To prove him false that says I love thee not.

DEMETR.　I say I love thee more than he can do.

LYSANDE.　If thou say so, withdraw, and prove it too.

DEMETR.　Quick, come.

HERMIA.　Lysander, whereto tends all this?

LYSANDE.　Away, you Ethiope!

赫米娅： 我不懂你说这种话的意思。

海丽娜： 好，尽管装腔下去，扮着这一副苦脸，等我一转背，就
要向我作嘴脸了；大家彼此眨眨眼睛，把这个绝妙的玩笑尽管
开下去吧，将来会记载在历史上的。假如你们是有同情心，懂
得礼貌的，就不该把我当做这样的笑柄。再会吧；一半也是我
自己不好，死别或生离不久便可以补赎我的错误。

拉山德： 不要走，温柔的海丽娜！听我解释。我的爱！我的生命！
我的灵魂！美丽的海丽娜！

海丽娜： 多好听的话！

赫米娅： 亲爱的，不要那样嘲笑她。

狄米特律斯： 要是她的恳求不能使你不说那种话，我将强迫你闭
住你的嘴。

拉山德： 她想恳求我，你想强迫我，可是都无济于事。你的威胁
正和她的软弱的祈告同样没有力量。海伦，我爱你！凭着我的
生命起誓，我爱你！谁说我不爱你的，我愿意用我的生命证明
他说谎；为了你我是乐意把生命捐弃的。

狄米特律斯： 我说我比他更要爱你得多。

拉山德： 要是你这样说，那么把剑拔出来证明一下吧。

狄米特律斯： 好，快些，来！

赫米娅： 拉山德，这一切究竟是怎么一回事呢？

拉山德： 走开，你这黑鬼！

DEMETR.　No, no, sir: – he will

　　Seem to break loose – take on as you would follow,

　　But yet come not. You are a tame man; go!

LYSANDE.　Hang off, thou˙cat, thou burr; vile thing, let loose,

　　Or I will shake thee from me like a serpent.

HERMIA.　Why are you grown so rude? What change is this, Sweet

　　love?

LYSANDE.　Thy love! Out, tawny Tartar, out!

　　Out, loathed medicine! O hated potion, hence!

HERMIA.　Do you not jest?

HELENA.　Yes, sooth; and so do you.

LYSANDE.　Demetrius, I will keep my word with thee.

DEMETR.　I would I had your bond; for I perceive

　　A weak bond holds you; I'll not trust your word.

LYSANDE.　What, should I hurt her, strike her, kill her dead?

　　Although I hate her, I'll not harm her so.

HERMIA.　What! Can you do me greater harm than hate?

　　Hate me! wherefore? O me! what news, my love?

　　Am not I Hermia? Are not you Lysander?

　　I am as fair now as I was erewhile.

　　Since night you loved me; yet since night you left me.

　　Why then, you left me – O, the gods forbid! –

　　In earnest, shall I say?

LYSANDE.　Ay, by my life!

　　And never did desire to see thee more.

　　Therefore be out of hope, of question, of doubt;

狄米特律斯： 不，不——你可不能骗我而自己逃走；假意说着来来，却在准备乘机溜去。你是个不中用的汉子，来吧！

拉山德： 放开手，你这猫！你这牛蒡子！贱东西，放开手！否则我要像摔掉身上一条蛇那样摔掉你了。

赫米娅： 为什么你变得这样凶暴？究竟是什么缘故呢，爱人？

拉山德： 你的爱人！走开，黑鞑子！走开！可厌的毒物，叫人恶心的东西，给我滚吧！

赫米娅： 你还是在开玩笑吗？

海丽娜： 是的，你也是在开玩笑。

拉山德： 狄米特律斯，我一定不失信于你。

狄米特律斯： 你的话可有些不能算数，因为人家的柔情在牵系住你。我可信不过你的话。

拉山德： 什么！难道要我伤害她、打她、杀死她吗？虽然我厌恨她，我还不至于这样残忍。

赫米娅： 啊！还有什么事情比之你厌恨我更残忍呢？厌恨我！为什么呢？天哪！究竟是怎么一回事呢，我的好人？难道我不是赫米娅了吗？难道你不是拉山德了吗？我现在生得仍旧跟以前一个样子。就在这一夜里你还曾爱过我；但就在这一夜里你离开了我。那么你真的——唉，天哪！——存心离开我吗？

拉山德： 一点不错，而且再不要看见你的脸了；因此你可以断了念头，不必疑心，我的话是千真万确的：我厌恨你，我爱海丽娜，一点不是开玩笑。

Be certain, nothing truer; 'tis no jest

That I do hate thee and love Helena.

HERMIA.　O me! you juggler! you canker-blossom!

You thief of love! What! Have you come by night,

And stol'n my love's heart from him?

HELENA.　Fine, in faith!

Have you no modesty, no maiden shame,

No touch of bashfulness? What! Will you tear

Impatient answers from my gentle tongue?

Fie, fie! you counterfeit, you puppet you!

HERMIA.　Puppet! why so? Ay, that way goes the game.

Now I perceive that she hath made compare

Between our statures; she hath urged her height;

And with her personage, her tall personage,

Her height, forsooth, she hath prevailed with him.

And are you grown so high in his esteem

Because I am so dwarfish and so low?

How low am I, thou painted maypole? Speak.

How low am I? I am not yet so low

But that my nails can reach unto thine eyes.

HELENA.　I pray you, though you mock me, gentlemen,

Let her not hurt me. I was never curst;

I have no gift at all in shrewishness;

I am a right maid for my cowardice;

Let her not strike me. You perhaps may think,

Because she is something lower than myself,

赫米娅：　天啊！你这骗子！你这花中的蛀虫！你这爱情的贼！哼！你乘着黑夜，悄悄地把我的爱人的心偷了去吗？

海丽娜：　真好！难道你一点女人家的羞耻都没有，一点不晓得难为情，不晓得自重了吗？哼！你一定要引得我破口说出难听的话来吗？哼！哼！你这装腔作势的人！你这给人家愚弄的小玩偶！

赫米娅：　小玩偶！噢，原来如此。现在我才明白了她为什么把她的身材跟我的比较；她自夸她生得长，用她那身材，那高高的身材，赢得了他的心。因为我生得矮小，所以他便把你看得高不可及了吗？我是怎样一个矮法？你这涂脂抹粉的花棒儿！请你说，我是怎样矮法？矮虽矮，我的指爪还挖得着你的眼珠哩！

海丽娜：　先生们，虽然你们都在嘲弄我，但我求你们别让她伤害我。我从来不曾使过性子；我也完全不懂得怎样跟人家闹架儿；我是一个胆小怕事的女子。不要让她打我。也许因为她比我矮些，你们就以为我打得过她吧。

That I can match her.

HERMIA.　Lower! hark, again.

HELENA.　Good Hermia, do not be so bitter with me.

I evermore did love you, Hermia,

Did ever keep your counsels, never wronged you;

Save that, in love unto Demetrius,

I told him of your stealth unto this wood.

He followed you; for love I followed him;

But he hath chid me hence, and threatened me

To strike me, spurn me, nay, to kill me too;

And now, so you will let me quiet go,

To Athens will I bear my folly back,

And follow you no further. Let me go.

You see how simple and how fond I am.

HERMIA.　Why, get you gone! Who is't that hinders you?

HELENA.　A foolish heart that I leave here behind.

HERMIA.　What! with Lysander?

HELENA.　With Demetrius

LYSANDE.　Be not afraid; she shall not harm thee, Helena.

DEMETR.　No, sir, she shall not, though you take her part.

HELENA.　O, when she is angry, she is keen and shrewd;

She was a vixen when she went to school;

And, though she be but little, she is fierce.

HERMIA.　Little again! Nothing but low and little!

Why will you suffer her to flout me thus?

Let me come to her.

赫米娅：　生得矮些！听，又来了！

海丽娜：　好赫米娅，不要对我这样凶！我一直是爱你的，赫米娅，
　　　　有什么事总跟你商量，从来不曾对你作过欺心的事；除了这次，
　　　　为了对于狄米特律斯的爱情的缘故，我把你私奔到这座林中的
　　　　事告诉了他。他追踪着你；为了爱，我又追踪着他；但他一直
　　　　是斥骂着我，威吓着我说要打我、踢我，甚至于要杀死我。现
　　　　在你让我悄悄地走了吧；我愿带着我的愚蠢回到雅典去，不再
　　　　跟着你们了。让我走；你瞧我是多么傻多么痴心！

赫米娅：　好，你走就走吧，谁在拦你？

海丽娜：　一颗发痴的心，但我把它丢弃在这里了。

赫米娅：　噢，给了拉山德了是不是？

海丽娜：　不，给了狄米特律斯。

拉山德：　不要怕，她不会伤害你的，海丽娜。

狄米特律斯：　当然不会的，先生；即使你帮着她也不要紧。

海丽娜：　啊，她一发起怒来，真是又凶又狠。在学校里她就是出
　　　　名的雌老虎；很小的时候便那么凶了。

赫米娅：　又是"很小"！老是矮啊小啊的说个不住！为什么你让
　　　　她这样讥笑我呢？让我跟她拼命去。

LYSANDE.　Get you gone, you dwarf;

　　You minimus, of hind'ring knot-grass made;

　　You bead, you acorn.

DEMETR.　You are too officious

　　In her behalf that scorns your services.

　　Let her alone; speak not of Helena;

　　Take not her part; for if thou dost intend

　　Never so little show of love to her,

　　Thou shalt aby it.

LYSANDE.　Now she holds me not.

　　Now follow, if thou dar'st, to try whose right,

　　Of thine or mine, is most in Helena.

DEMETR.　Follow! Nay, I'll go with thee, cheek by jowl.

[*Exeunt Lysander and Demetrius.*]

HERMIA.　You, mistress, all this coil is long of you.

　　Nay, go not back.

HELENA.　I will not trust you, I;

　　Nor longer stay in your curst company.

　　Your hands than mine are quicker for a fray;

　　My legs are longer though, to run away.

　　[*Exit.*]

HERMIA.　I am amazed, and know not what to say.

　　[*Exit.*]

拉山德：　滚开，你这矮子！你这发育不全的三寸丁！你这小珠子！你这小青豆！

狄米特律斯：　她用不着你帮忙，因此不必那样乱献殷勤。让她去；不许你嘴里再提到海丽娜，不要你来给她撑腰。要是你再向她略献殷勤，就请你当心着吧！

拉山德：　现在她已经不再拉住我了；你要是有胆子，跟我来吧，我们倒要试试看究竟海丽娜该属于谁。

狄米特律斯：　跟你来！嘿，我要和你并着肩走呢。

（拉山德、狄米特律斯二人下。）

赫米娅：　你，小姐，这一切的纷扰都是因为你的缘故。哎，别逃啊！

海丽娜：　我怕你，我不敢跟脾气这么大的你在一起。打起架来，你的手比我快得多；但我的腿比你长些，逃起来你追不上我。（下。）

赫米娅：　我简直莫名其妙，不知道说些什么话好。（下。）

OBERON.　This is thy negligence. Still thou mistak'st,

　　Or else committ'st thy knaveries wilfully.

PUCK.　Believe me, king of shadows, I mistook.

　　Did not you tell me I should know the man

　　By the Athenian garments he had on?

　　And so far blameless proves my enterprise

　　That I have 'nointed an Athenian's eyes;

　　And so far am I glad it so did sort,

　　As this their jangling I esteem a sport.

OBERON.　Thou seest these lovers seek a place to fight.

　　Hie therefore, Robin, overcast the night;

　　The starry welkin cover thou anon

　　With drooping fog as black as Acheron,

　　And lead these testy rivals so astray

　　As one come not within another's way.

　　Like to Lysander sometime frame thy tongue,

　　Then stir Demetrius up with bitter wrong;

　　And sometime rail thou like Demetrius;

　　And from each other look thou lead them thus,

　　Till o'er their brows death-counterfeiting sleep

　　With leaden legs and batty wings doth creep.

　　Then crush this herb into Lysander's eye;

　　Whose liquor hath this virtuous property,

　　To take from thence all error with his might

　　And make his eyeballs roll with wonted sight.

　　When they next wake, all this derision

奥布朗：　这是你的大意所致；要不是你弄错了，一定是你故意在捣蛋。

迫克：　相信我，仙王，是我弄错了。你不是对我说只要认清楚那人穿着雅典人的衣裳？照这样说起来我完全不曾错，因为我是把花汁滴在一个雅典人的眼上。事情会弄到这样我是满快活的，因为他们的吵闹看着怪有趣味。

奥布朗：　你瞧这两个恋人找地方决斗去了，因此，罗宾，快去把夜天遮暗了；你就去用像冥河的水一样黑的浓雾盖住了星空，再引这两个声势汹汹的仇人迷失了路，不要让他们碰在一起。有时你学着拉山德的声音痛骂狄米特律斯，叫他气得直跳，有时学着狄米特律斯的样子斥责拉山德：用这种法子把他们两个分开，直到他们奔波得精疲力竭，死一样的睡眠拖着铅样沉重的腿和蝙蝠的翅膀爬上了他们的额上；然后你把这草挤出汁来涂在拉山德的眼睛上，它能够解去一切的错误，使他的眼睛恢复从前的眼光。等他们醒来之后，这一切的戏谑，就会像是一场梦境或是空虚的幻想；一班恋人们便将回到雅典去，而且将订下白头到老、永无尽期的盟约。在我差遣你去作这件事的时候，我要去访问我的王后，向她讨那个印度孩子；然后我要解除她眼中所见的怪物的幻觉，一切事情都将和平解决。

Shall seem a dream and fruitless vision;

And back to Athens shall the lovers wend

With league whose date till death shall never end.

Whiles I in this affair do thee employ,

I'll to my queen, and beg her Indian boy;

And then I will her charmed eye release

From monster's view, and all things shall be peace.

PUCK.   My fairy lord, this must be done with haste,

For night's swift dragons cut the clouds full fast;

And yonder shines Aurora's harbinger,

At whose approach ghosts, wandering here and there,

Troop home to churchyards. Damned spirits all

That in cross-ways and floods have burial,

Already to their wormy beds are gone,

For fear lest day should look their shames upon;

They wilfully themselves exiled from light,

And must for aye consort with black-browed night.

OBERON.   But we are spirits of another sort:

I with the Morning's love have oft made sport;

And, like a forester, the groves may tread

Even till the eastern gate, all fiery red,

Opening on Neptune with fair blessed beams,

Turns into yellow gold his salt green streams.

But, notwithstanding, haste, make no delay;

We may effect this business yet ere day.

[*Exit.*]

迫克：　这事我们必须赶早办好，主公，

　　　　因为黑夜已经驾起他的飞龙；

　　　　晨星，黎明的先驱，已照亮苍穹；

　　　　一个个鬼魂四散地奔返殡宫：

　　　　还有那横死的幽灵抱恨长终，

　　　　道旁水底有他们的白骨成丛，

　　　　为怕白昼揭露了丑恶的形容，

　　　　早已向重泉归寝，相伴着蛆虫；

　　　　他们永远见不到日光的融融，

　　　　只每夜在暗野里凭吊着凄风。

奥布朗：　但你我可完全不能比并他们；

　　　　晨光中我惯和猎人一起游巡，

　　　　如同林居人一样踏访着丛林：

　　　　即使东方开启了火红的天门，

　　　　大海上照耀万道灿烂的光针，

　　　　青碧的大海化成了一片黄金。

　　　　但我们应该早早办好这事情，

　　　　最好别把它迁延着直到天明。

　　　　（下。）

PUCK.   Up and down, up and down,

　　I will lead them up and down.

　　I am feared in field and town.

　　Goblin, lead them up and down.

　　Here comes one.

[*Enter Lysander.*]

LYSANDE.   Where art thou, proud Demetrius? Speak thou now.

PUCK.   Here, villain, drawn and ready. Where art thou?

LYSANDE.   I will be with thee straight.

PUCK.   Follow me, then,

　　To plainer ground

　　[*Exit Lysander.*]

[*Enter Demetrius.*]

DEMETR.   Lysander, speak again.

　　Thou runaway, thou coward, art thou fled?

　　Speak! In some bush? Where dost thou hide thy head?

PUCK.   Thou coward, art thou bragging to the stars,

　　Telling the bushes that thou look'st for wars,

　　And wilt not come? Come, recreant, come, thou child;

　　I'll whip thee with a rod. He is defiled

　　That draws a sword on thee.

DEMETR.   Yea, art thou there?

迫克：　奔到这边来，奔过那边去；

我要领他们，奔来又奔去。

林间和市上，无人不怕我；

我要领他们，走尽林中路。

这儿来了一个。

（拉山德重上。）

拉山德：　你在哪里，骄傲的狄米特律斯？说出来！

迫克：　在这儿，恶徒！把你的剑拔出来准备着吧。你在哪里？

拉山德：　我立刻就过来。

迫克：　那么跟我来吧，到平坦一点的地方。（拉山德随声音下。）

（狄米特律斯重上。）

狄米特律斯：　拉山德，你再开口啊！你逃走了，你这懦夫！你逃
　　　走了吗？说话呀！躲在那一堆树丛里吗？你躲在哪里呀？

迫克：　你这懦夫！你在向星星们夸口，向树林子挑战，但是却不
　　　敢过来吗？来，卑怯汉！来，你这小孩子！我要好好抽你一顿。
　　　谁要跟你比剑才真倒霉！

狄米特律斯：　呀，你在那边吗？

PUCK.　Follow my voice; we'll try no manhood here.

　　[*Exeunt.*]

[*Re-enter Lysander.*]

LYSANDE.　He goes before me, and still dares me on;

　　When I come where he calls, then he is gone.

　　The villain is much lighter heeled than I.

　　I followed fast, but faster he did fly,

　　That fallen am I in dark uneven way,

　　And here will rest me.

　　[*Lies down.*] Come, thou gentle day!

　　For if but once thou show me thy grey light,

　　I'll find Demetrius, and revenge this spite

　　[*Sleeps.*]

[*Re-enter Puck and Demetrius.*]

PUCK.　Ho, ho, ho! Coward, why com'st thou not?

DEMETR.　Abide me, if thou dar'st; for well I wot

　　Thou run'st before me, shifting every place,

　　And dar'st not stand, nor look me in the face.

　　Where art thou now?

PUCK.　Come hither; I am here.

DEMETR.　Nay, then, thou mock'st me. Thou shalt buy this dear,

　　If ever I thy face by daylight see;

　　Now, go thy way. Faintness constraineth me

迫克：　跟我的声音来吧；这儿不是适宜我们战斗的地方。（同下。）

（拉山德重上。）

拉山德：　他走在我的前头，老是挑拨着我上前；一等我走到他叫喊着的地方，他又早已不在。这个坏蛋比我脚步快得多，我追得快，他可逃得更快，使我在黑暗崎岖的路上绊了一跤。让我在这儿休息一下吧。（躺下。）来吧，你仁心的白昼！只要你一露出你的一线灰白的微光，我就可以看见狄米特律斯而洗雪这次仇恨了。（睡去。）

（迫克及狄米特律斯重上。）

迫克：　哈！哈！哈！懦夫！你为什么不来？

狄米特律斯：　要是你有胆量的话，等着我吧；我全然明白你跑在我前面，从这儿窜到那儿，不敢站住，也不敢见我的面。你现在是在什么地方？

迫克：　过来，我在这儿。

狄米特律斯：　哼，你在摆布我。要是天亮了我看见你的面孔，你好好地留点儿神；现在，去你的吧！疲乏逼着我倒下在这寒冷的地上，等候着白天的降临。（躺下睡去。）

To measure out my length on this cold bed.

By day's approach look to be visited.

[*Lies down and sleeps.*]

[*Enter Helena.*]

HELENA.   O weary night, O long and tedious night,

Abate thy hours! Shine comforts from the east,

That I may back to Athens by daylight,

From these that my poor company detest.

And sleep, that sometimes shuts up sorrow's eye,

Steal me awhile from mine own company.

[*Sleeps.*]

PUCK.   Yet but three? Come one more;

Two of both kinds makes up four.

Here she comes, curst and sad.

Cupid is a knavish lad,

Thus to make poor females mad.

[*Enter Hermia.*]

HERMIA.   Never so weary, never so in woe,

Bedabbled with the dew, and torn with briers,

I can no further crawl, no further go;

My legs can keep no pace with my desires.

Here will I rest me till the break of day.

Heavens shield Lysander, if they mean a fray!

[*Lies down.*]

（海丽娜重上。）

海丽娜：　疲乏的夜啊！冗长的夜啊！减少一些你的时辰吧！从东
　　　　方出来的安慰，快照耀起来吧！好让我借着晨光回到雅典去，
　　　　离开这一群人，他们大家都讨厌着可怜的我。慈悲的睡眠，有
　　　　时你闭上了悲伤的眼睛，求你暂时让我忘却了自己的存在吧！
　　　　（躺下睡去。）

迫克：　两男加两女，四个无错误；
　　　　三人已在此，一人在何处？
　　　　哈哈她来了，满脸愁云罩：
　　　　爱神真不好，惯惹人烦恼！

（赫米娅重上。）

赫米娅：　从来不曾这样疲乏过，从来不曾这样伤心过！我的身上
　　　　沾满了露水，我的衣裳被荆棘所抓破；我跑也跑不动，爬也爬
　　　　不动了；我的两条腿再也不能听从我的心愿。让我在这儿休息
　　　　一下以待天明。要是他们真要决斗的话，愿天保佑拉山德吧！
　　　　（躺下睡去。）

PUCK.　　On the ground

　　　　Sleep sound;

　　　　I'll apply

　　　　To your eye,

　　　　Gentle lover, remedy.

　　　　[*Squeezing the juice on Lysander's eyes.*]

　　　　When thou wak'st,

　　　　Thou tak'st

　　　　True delight

　　　　In the sight

　　　　Of thy former lady's eye;

　　　　And the country proverb known,

　　　　That every man should take his own,

　　　　In your waking shall be shown:

　　　　Jack shall have Jill;

　　　　Nought shall go ill;

　　　　The man shall have his mare again, and all shall be well.

　　　　[*Exit.*]

迫克：　梦将残，睡方酣，

　　　　神仙药，祛幻觉，

　　　　百般迷梦全消却。

　　　　（挤草汁于拉山德眼上。）

　　　　醒眼见，旧人脸，

　　　　乐满心，情不禁，

　　　　从此欢爱复深深。

　　　　一句俗语说得好，

　　　　各人各有各的宝，

　　　　等你醒来就知道：

　　　　哥儿爱姐儿，

　　　　两两无参差；

　　　　失马复得马，

　　　　一场大笑话！

　　　　（下。）

ACT IV   SCENE I

The wood. Lysander, Demetrius,Helena, and Hermia, lying asleep.
[Enter Titania and Bottom, and other Fairies attending;Oberon behind,
unseen.]

TITANIA.   Come, sit thee down upon this flowery bed,

While I thy amiable cheeks do coy,

And stick musk-roses in thy sleek smooth head,

And kiss thy fair large ears, my gentle joy.

BOTTOM.   Where's Peasblossom?

PEASE.   Ready.

BOTTOM.   Scratch my head, Peasblossom. – Where's Mounsieur
Cobweb?

COBWEB.   Ready.

BOTTOM.   Mounsieur Cobweb; good mounsieur, get you your
weapons in your hand and kill me a red-hipped humble-bee on the
top of a thistle; and, good mounsieur, bring me the honey-bag. Do
not fret yourself too much in the action, mounsieur; and, good
mounsieur, have a care the honey-bag break not; I would be loath
to have you over-flown with a honey-bag, signior.

Where's Mounsieur Mustardseed?

MUSTARD.   Ready.

第四幕　第一场

林中。拉山德、狄米特律斯、海丽娜、赫米娅酣睡未醒。
（提泰妮娅及波顿上，众仙随侍；奥布朗潜随其后。）

提泰妮娅：　来，坐下在这花床上。我要爱抚你的可爱的脸颊；我
　　　要把麝香玫瑰插在你柔软光滑的头颅上；我要吻你的美丽的大
　　　耳朵，我的温柔的宝贝！

波顿：　豆花呢？

豆花：　有。

波顿：　替咱把头搔搔，豆花儿。蛛网先生在哪儿？

蛛网：　有。

波顿：　蛛网先生，好先生，把您的刀拿好，替咱把那蓟草叶尖上
　　　的红屁股的野蜂儿杀了；然后，好先生，替咱把蜜囊儿拿来。
　　　干那事的时候可别太性急，先生；而且，好先生，当心别把蜜
　　　囊儿给弄破了；要是您在蜜囊里头淹死了，那咱可不很乐意，
　　　先生。芥子先生在哪儿？

芥子：　有。

BOTTOM.　Give me your neif, Mounsieur Mustardseed.

Pray you, leave your curtsy, good mounsieur.

MUSTARD.　What's your will?

BOTTOM.　Nothing, good mounsieur, but to help Cavalero Cobweb to scratch. I must to the barber's, mounsieur; for methinks I am marvelous hairy about the face; and I am such a tender ass, if my hair do but tickle me I must scratch.

TITANIA.　What, wilt thou hear some music, my sweet love?

BOTTOM.　I have a reasonable good ear in music. Let's have the tongs and the bones.

TITANIA.　Or say, sweet love, what thou desirest to eat.

BOTTOM.　Truly, a peck of provender; I could munch your good dry oats. Methinks I have a great desire to a bottle of hay. Good hay, sweet hay, hath no fellow.

TITANIA.　I have a venturous fairy that shall seek

The squirrel's hoard, and fetch thee new nuts.

BOTTOM.　I had rather have a handful or two of dried peas.

But, I pray you, let none of your people stir me; I have an exposition of sleep come upon me.

TITANIA.　Sleep thou, and I will wind thee in my arms.

Fairies, be gone, and be all ways away. [*Exeunt Fairies.*]

So doth the woodbine the sweet honeysuckle

Gently entwist; – the female ivy so

Enrings the barky fingers of the elm.

O, how I love thee! how I dote on thee!

[*They sleep.*]

波顿：　把您的小手儿给我，芥子先生。请您不要多礼吧，好先生。

芥子：　你有什么吩咐？
波顿：　没有什么，好先生，只是帮蛛网骑士替咱搔搔痒。咱一定得理发去，先生，因为咱觉得脸上毛得很。咱是一头感觉非常灵敏的驴子，要是一根毛把咱触痒了，咱就非得搔一下子不可。

提泰妮娅：　你要不要听一些音乐，我的好人？
波顿：　咱很懂得一点儿音乐。咱们来一下子锣鼓吧。

提泰妮娅：　好人，你要吃些什么呢？
波顿：　真的，来一堆刍秣吧；您要是有好的干麦秆，也可以给咱大嚼一顿。咱想，咱怪想吃那么一捆干草；好干草，美味的干草，什么也比不上它。
提泰妮娅：　我有一个善于冒险的小神仙，可以给你到松鼠的仓里取些新鲜的榛栗来。
波顿：　咱宁可吃一把两把干豌豆。但是谢谢您，吩咐您那些人们别惊动咱吧，咱想要睡他妈的一觉。

提泰妮娅：　睡吧，我要把你抱在我的臂中。神仙们，往各处散开去吧。（众仙下。）菟丝也正是这样温柔地缠附着芬芳的金银花；女萝也正是这样缱绻着榆树的皱折的臂枝。啊，我是多么爱你！我是多么热恋着你！（同睡去。）

[*Enter Puck.*]

OBERON. [*Advancing*] Welcome, good Robin. Seest thou this sweet
   sight?
   Her dotage now I do begin to pity;
   For, meeting her of late behind the wood,
   Seeking sweet favours for this hateful fool,
   I did upbraid her and fall out with her.
   For she his hairy temples then had rounded
   With coronet of fresh and fragrant flowers;
   And that same dew which sometime on the buds
   Was wont to swell like round and orient pearls
   Stood now within the pretty flowerets' eyes,
   Like tears that did their own disgrace bewail.
   When I had at my pleasure taunted her,
   And she in mild terms begged my patience,
   I then did ask of her her changeling child;
   Which straight she gave me, and her fairy sent
   To bear him to my bower in fairy land.
   And now I have the boy, I will undo
   This hateful imperfection of her eyes.
   And, gentle Puck, take this transformed scalp
   From off the head of this Athenian swain,
   That he awaking when the other do
   May all to Athens back again repair,
   And think no more of this night's accidents

（迫克上。）

奥布朗： （上前。）欢迎，好罗宾！你见没见这种可爱的情景？我对于她的痴恋开始有点不忍了。刚才我在树林后面遇见她正在为这个可憎的蠢货找寻爱情的礼物，我就谴责她，跟她争吵起来，因为那时她把芬芳的鲜花制成花环，环绕着他那毛茸茸的额角；原来在嫩芯上晶莹饱满、如同东方的明珠一样的露水，如今却含在那一朵朵美艳的小花的眼中，像是盈盈欲泣的眼泪，痛心着它们所受的耻辱。我把她尽情嘲骂一番之后，她低声下气地请求我息怒，于是我便乘机向她索讨那个换儿；她立刻把他给了我，差她的仙侍把他送到了我的寝宫。现在我已经把这个孩子弄到手，我将解去她眼中这种可憎的迷惑。好迫克，你去把这雅典村夫头上的变形的头盖揭下，等他和大家一同醒来的时候，好让他回到雅典去，把这晚间发生的一切事情只当作一场梦魇。但是先让我给仙后解去了魔法吧。（以草触她的眼睛。）回复你原来的本性，解去你眼前的幻景；这一朵女贞花采自月姊园庭，它会使爱情的小卉失去功能。喂，我的提泰妮娅，醒醒吧，我的好王后！

But as the fierce vexation of a dream.

But first I will release the Fairy Queen.

Be as thou wast wont to be;

[*Touching her eyes with an herb.*]

See as thou was wont to see.

Dian's bud o'er Cupid's flower

Hath such force and blessed power.

Now, my Titania; wake you, my sweet queen

TITANIA.　My Oberon! What visions have I seen!

Methought I was enamoured of an ass.

OBERON.　There lies your love.

TITANIA.　How came these things to pass?

O, how mine eyes do loathe his visage now!

OBERON.　Silence awhile. Robin, take off this head.

Titania, music call; and strike more dead

Than common sleep of all these five the sense.

TITANIA.　Music, ho, music, such as charmeth sleep! [*Music, still.*]

PUCK.　Now when thou wak'st with thine own fool's eyes peep.

OBERON.　Sound, music! – Come, my Queen, take hands with me,

And rock the ground whereon these sleepers be.

Now thou and I are new in amity,

And will to-morrow midnight solemnly

Dance in Duke Theseus' house triumphantly,

And bless it to all fair prosperity.

There shall the pairs of faithful lovers be

Wedded, with Theseus, an in jollity.

提泰妮娅：　我的奥布朗！我看见了怎样的幻景！好像我爱上了一头驴子啦。

奥布朗：　那边就是你的爱人。

提泰妮娅：　这一切事情怎么会发生的呢？啊，现在我看见他的样子是多么惹气！

奥布朗：　静一会儿。罗宾，把他的头壳揭下了。提泰妮娅，叫他们奏起音乐来吧，让这五个人睡得全然失去了知觉。

提泰妮娅：　来，奏起催眠的乐声柔婉！（音乐。）

迫克：　等你一觉醒来，蠢汉，用你的傻眼睛瞧看。

奥布朗：　奏下去，音乐！来，我的王后，让我们携手同行，让我们的舞蹈震动这些人睡着的地面。现在我们已经言归于好，明天夜半将要一同到忒修斯公爵的府中跳着庄严的欢舞，祝福他家繁荣昌盛。这两对忠心的恋人也将在那里和忒修斯同时举行婚礼，大家心中充满了喜乐。

PUCK.　　Fairy King, attend and mark;

　　　I do hear the morning lark.

OBERON.　　Then, my Queen, in silence sad,

　　　Trip we after night's shade.

　　　We the globe can compass soon,

　　　Swifter than the wangdering moon.

TITANIA.　　Come, my lord; and in our flight,

　　　Tell me how it came this night

　　　That I sleeping here was found

　　　With these mortals on the ground.

　　　[*Exeunt. Wind horns.*]

[*Enter Theseus, Hippolyta, Egeus, and Train.*]

THESEUS.　　Go, one of you, find out the forester; –

　　　For now our observation is performed,

　　　And since we have the vaward of the day,

　　　My love shall hear the music of my hounds.

　　　Uncouple in the western valley; let them go.

　　　Despatch, I say, and find the forester. –

　　　We will, fair Queen, up to the mountain's top,

　　　And mark the musical confusion

　　　Of hounds and echo in conjunction.

HIPPOLYTA.　　I was with Hercules and Cadmus once

　　　When in a wood of Crete they bayed the bear

　　　With hounds of Sparta; never did I hear

迫克：　仙王，仙王，留心听，

　　　　我听见云雀歌吟。

奥布朗：　王后，让我们静静

　　　　追随着夜的踪影；

　　　　我们环绕着地球，

　　　　快过明月的光流。

提泰妮娅：　夫君，请你在一路

　　　　告诉我一切缘故，

　　　　这些人来自何方，

　　　　当我熟睡的时光。

　　　　（同下。幕内号角声。）

（忒修斯、希波吕忒、伊吉斯及侍从等上。）

忒修斯：　你们中间谁去把猎奴唤来。我们已把五月节的仪式遵行，

　　　　现在才只是清晨，我的爱人应当听一听猎犬的音乐。把它们放

　　　　在西面的山谷里；快去把猎奴唤来。美丽的王后，让我们到山

　　　　顶上去，领略着猎犬们的吠叫和山谷中的回声应和在一起的妙

　　　　乐吧。

希波吕忒：　我曾经同赫刺克勒斯和卡德摩斯[1]一起在克里特林中

　　　　行猎，他们用斯巴达的猎犬追赶着巨熊，那种雄壮的吠声我真

---

[1] 卡德摩斯（Cadmus），希腊神话中的英雄，忒拜城的创建者。

Such gallant chiding, for, besides the groves,

The skies, the fountains, every region near

Seemed all one mutual cry. I never heard

So musical a discord, such sweet thunder.

THESEUS.　My hounds are bred out of the Spartan kind,

So flewed, so sanded; and their heads are hung

With ears that sweep away the morning dew;

Crook-kneed and dew-lapped like Thessalian bulls;

Slow in pursuit, but matched in mouth like bells,

Was never hollaed to, nor cheered with horn,

Each under each. A cry more tuneable

In Crete, in Sparta, nor in Thessaly.

Judge when you hear. But, soft, what nymphs are these?

EGEUS.　My lord, this is my daughter here asleep,

And this Lysander, this Demetrius is,

This Helena, old Nedar's Helena.

I wonder of their being here together.

THESEUS.　No doubt they rose up early to observe

The rite of May; and, hearing our intent,

Came here in grace of our solemnity.

But speak, Egeus; is not this the day

That Hermia should give answer of her choice?

EGEUS.　It is, my lord.

THESEUS.　Go, bid the huntsmen wake them with their horns.

[*Horns, and they wake. Shout within, and they all start up.*]

Good-morrow, friends. Saint Valentine is past;

是第一次听到；除了丛林之外，天空和群山，以及一切附近的区域，似乎混成了一片交互的呐喊。我从来不曾听见过那样谐美的喧声，那样悦耳的雷鸣。

忒修斯：　我的猎犬也是斯巴达种，一样的颊肉下垂，一样的黄沙的毛色；它们的头上垂着两片挥拂晨露的耳朵；它们的膝骨是弯曲的，并且像忒萨利亚种的公牛一样喉头长着垂肉。它们在追逐时不很迅速，但它们的吠声彼此高下相应，就像钟声那样合调。无论在克里特、斯巴达或是忒萨利亚，都不曾有过这么一队猎狗，应和着猎人的号角和呼召，吠得这样好听；你听见了之后便可以自己判断。但是且慢！这些都是什么仙女？

伊吉斯：　殿下，这儿躺着的是我的女儿；这是拉山德；这是狄米特律斯；这是海丽娜，奈达老人的女儿。我不知道他们怎么都在这儿。

忒修斯：　他们一定早起守五月节，因为闻知了我们的意旨，所以赶到这儿来参加我们的典礼。但是，伊吉斯，今天不是赫米娅应该决定她的选择的日子吗？

伊吉斯：　是的，殿下。

忒修斯：　去，叫猎奴们吹起号角来惊醒他们。（幕内号角及呐喊声；拉山德、狄米特律斯、赫米娅、海丽娜四人惊醒跳起。）早安，朋友们！情人节早已过去了，你们这一辈林鸟到现在才

Begin these wood-birds but to couple now?

LYSANDE.　Pardon, my lord.

　　[*He and the rest kneel to Theseus.*]

THESEUS.　I pray you all, stand up

　　　I know you two are rival enemies;

　　　How comes this gentle concord in the world

　　　That hatred is so far from jealousy

　　　To sleep by hate, and fear no enmity?

LYSANDE.　My lord, I shall reply amazedly,

　　　Half sleep, half waking; but as yet, I swear,

　　　I cannot truly say how I came here,

　　　But, as I think – for truly would I speak,

　　　And now I do bethink me, so it is –

　　　I came with Hermia hither. Our intent

　　　Was to be gone from Athens, where we might,

　　　Without the peril of the Athenian law –

EGEUS.　Enough, enough, my Lord; you have enough;

　　　I beg the law, the law upon his head.

　　　They would have stol'n away, they would, Demetrius,

　　　Thereby to have defeated you and me:

　　　You of your wife, and me of my consent,

　　　Of my consent that she should be your wife.

DEMETR.　My lord, fair Helen told me of their stealth,

　　　Of this their purpose hither to this wood;

　　　And I in fury hither followed them,

　　　Fair Helena in fancy following me.

配起对来吗？

拉山德：　请殿下恕罪！

（偕余人并跪下。）

忒修斯：　请你们站起来吧。我知道你们两人是对头冤家，怎么会变得这样和气，大家睡在一块儿，没有一点猜忌，再不怕敌人了呢？

拉山德：　殿下，我现在还是糊里糊涂，不知道应当怎样回答您的问话；但是我敢发誓说我真的不知道怎么会在这儿；但是我想——我要说老实话，我现在记起来了，一点不错，我是和赫米娅一同到这儿来的；我们想要逃出雅典，避过了雅典法律的峻严，我们便可以——

伊吉斯：　够了，够了，殿下；话已经说得够了。我要求依法，依法惩办他。他们打算，他们打算逃走，狄米特律斯，他们打算用那种手段欺弄我们，使你的妻子落空，使我给你的允许也落空。

狄米特律斯：　殿下，海丽娜告诉了我他们的出奔，告诉了我他们到这儿林中来的目的；我在盛怒之下追踪他们，同时海丽娜因为痴心的缘故也追踪着我。但是，殿下，我不知道什么一种力量——但一定是有一种力量——使我对于赫米娅的爱情会像

But, my good lord, I wot not by what power –

But by some power it is – my love to Hermia,

Melted as the snow, seems to me now

As the remembrance of an idle gaud

Which in my childhood I did dote upon;

And all the faith, the virtue of my heart,

The object and the pleasure of mine eye,

Is only Helena. To her, my lord,

Was I betrothed ere I saw Hermia.

But, like a sickness, did I loathe this food;

But, as in health, come to my natural taste,

Now I do wish it, love it, long for it,

And will for evermore be true to it.

THESEUS.　　Fair lovers, you are fortunately met;

Of this discourse we more will hear anon.

Egeus, I will overbear your will;

For in the temple, by and by, with us

These couples shall eternally be knit.

And, for the morning now is something worn,

Our purposed hunting shall be set aside.

Away with us to Athens, three and three;

We'll hold a feast in great solemnity.

Come, Hippolyta.

[*Exeunt Theseus, Hippolyta, Egeus.*]

霜雪一样溶解,现在想起来,就像回忆一段童年时所爱好的一件玩物一样;我一切的忠信、一切的心思、一切乐意的眼光,都是属于海丽娜一个人了。我在没有认识赫米娅之前,殿下,就已经和她订过盟约;但正如一个人在生病的时候一样,我厌弃着这一道珍馐,等到健康恢复,就会回复正常的胃口。现在我希求着她,珍爱着她,思慕着她,将要永远忠心于她。

忒修斯:　　俊美的恋人们,我们相遇得很巧;等会儿我们便可以再听你们把这段话讲下去。伊吉斯,你的意志只好屈服一下了;这两对少年不久便将跟我们一起在神庙中缔结永久的鸳盟。现在清晨快将过去,我们本来准备的行猎只好中止。跟我们一起到雅典去吧;三三成对地,我们将要大张盛宴。来,希波吕忒。

(忒修斯、希波吕忒、伊吉斯及侍从下。)

DEMETR.   These things seem small and undistinguishable,

Like far-off mountains turned into clouds.

HERMIA.   Methinks I see these things with parted eye,

When every thing seems double.

HELENA.   So methinks;

And I have found Demetrius like a jewel,

Mine own, and not mine own.

DEMETR.   Are you sure

That we are awake? It seems to me

That yet we sleep, we dream. Do not you think

The Duke was here, and bid us follow him?

HERMIA.   Yea, and my father.

HELENA.   And Hippolyta.

LYSANDE.   And he did bid us follow to the temple.

DEMETR.   Why, then, we are awake; let's follow him;

And by the way let us recount our dreams.

[*Exeunt.*]

BOTTOM.   [*Awaking.*] When my cue comes, call me, and I will

answer. My next is Most fair Pyramus. Heigh-ho! Peter Quince!

Flute, the bellows-mender! Snout, the tinker! Starveling! God's

my life, stolen hence, and left me asleep! I have had a most rare

vision. I have had a dream, past the wit of man to say what dream

it was. Man is but an ass if he go about to expound this dream.

Methought I was – there is no man can tell what. Methought I was,

and methought I had, but man is but a patched fool, if he will

狄米特律斯：　这些事情似乎微细而无从捉摸，好像化为云雾的远
　　　山一样。

赫米娅：　我觉得好像这些事情我都用昏花的眼睛看着，一切都化
　　　作了层叠的两重似的。

海丽娜：　我也是这样想。我得到了狄米特律斯，像是得到了一颗
　　　宝石，好像是我自己的，又好像不是我自己的。

狄米特律斯：　你们真能断定我们现在是醒着吗？我觉得我们还是
　　　在睡着做梦。你们是不是以为公爵方才在这儿，叫我们跟他走
　　　吗？

赫米娅：　是的，我的父亲也在。

海丽娜：　还有希波吕忒。

拉山德：　他确曾叫我们跟他到神庙里去。

狄米特律斯：　那么我们真的已经醒了。让我们跟着他走；一路上
　　　讲着我们的梦。（同下。）

波顿：　（醒。）轮到咱说尾白的时候，请你们叫咱一声，咱就会答
　　　应；咱下面的一句是，"最美丽的皮拉摩斯。"喂！喂！彼得·昆
　　　斯！弗鲁特，修风箱的！斯诺特，补锅子的！斯塔佛林！他妈
　　　的！悄悄地溜走了，把咱撇下在这儿一个人睡觉吗？咱看见了
　　　一个奇怪得了不得的幻象，咱做了一个梦。没有人说得出那是
　　　怎样的一个梦；要是谁想把这个梦解释一下，那他一定是一头
　　　驴子。咱好像是——没有人说得出那是什么东西；咱好像是——
　　　咱好像有——但要是谁敢说出来咱好像有什么东西，那他一定

offer to say what methought I had. The eye of man hath not heard, the ear of man hath not seen, man's hand is not able to taste, his tongue to conceive, nor his heart to report, what my dream was. I will get Peter Quince to write a ballad of this dream. It shall be called Bottom's Dream, because it hath no bottom; and I will sing it in the latter end of a play, before the Duke. Peradventure, to make it the more gracious, I shall sing it at her death.

[*Exit.*]

是一个蠢材。咱那个梦啊，人们的眼睛从来没有听到过，人们的耳朵从来没有看见过，人们的手也尝不出来是什么味道，人们的舌头也想不出来是什么道理，人们的心也说不出来究竟那是怎样的一个梦。咱要叫彼得·昆斯给咱写一首歌儿咏一下这个梦，题目就叫做"波顿的梦"，因为这个梦可没有个底儿[1]；咱要在演完戏之后当着公爵大人的面前唱这个歌——或者更好些，还是等咱死了之后再唱吧。（下。）

---

[1] 波顿，原文Bottom，意为"底"，这里是一句双关语。

ACT IV   SCENE II

Athens. Quince's house.
[Enter Quince, Flute, Snout, and Starveling.]

QUINCE.   Have you sent to Bottom's house? Is he come home yet?

STARV.   He cannot be heard of. Out of doubt he is transported.

FLUTE.   If he come not, then the play is marred; it goes not forward, doth it?

QUINCE.   It is not possible. You have not a man in all Athens able to discharge Pyramus but he.

FLUTE.   No; he hath simply the best wit of any handicraft man in Athens.

QUINCE.   Yea, and the best person too; and he is a very paramour for a sweet voice.

FLUTE.   You must say paragon. A paramour is –
God bless us! – A thing of naught.

[Enter Snug.]

SNUG.   Masters, the Duke is coming from the temple; and there is two or three lords and ladies more married. If our sport had gone forward, we had all been made men.

第四幕　第二场

雅典。昆斯家中。

（昆斯、弗鲁特、斯诺特、斯塔佛林上。）

昆斯：　你们差人到波顿家里去过了吗？他还没有回家吗？

斯塔佛林：　一点消息都没有。他准是给妖精拐了去了。

弗鲁特：　要是他不回来，那么咱们的戏就要搁起来啦；它不能再演下去，是不是？

昆斯：　那当然演不下去罗；整个雅典城里除了他之外就没有第二个人可以演皮拉摩斯。

弗鲁特：　谁也演不了；他在雅典手艺人中间简直是最聪明的一个。

昆斯：　对，而且也是顶好的人；他有一副好喉咙，吊起膀子来真是顶呱呱的。

弗鲁特：　你说错了，你应当说"吊嗓子"。吊膀子，老天爷！那是一件难为情的事。

（斯纳格上。）

斯纳格：　列位，公爵大人刚从神庙里出来，还有两三位贵人和小姐们也在同时结了婚。要是咱们的玩意儿能够干下去，咱们一定大家都有好处。

FLUTE. O sweet bully Bottom! Thus hath he lost sixpence a day during his life; he could not have 'scaped sixpence a day. An the Duke had not given him sixpence a day for playing Pyramus, I'll be hanged. He would have deserved it: sixpence a day in Pyramus, or nothing.

[*Enter Bottom.*]

BOTTOM. Where are these lads? Where are these hearts?

QUINCE. Bottom! O most courageous day! O most happy hour!

BOTTOM. Masters, I am to discourse wonders; but ask me not what; for if I tell you, I am not true Athenian. I will tell you everything, right as it fell out.

QUINCE. Let us hear, sweet Bottom.

BOTTOM. Not a word of me. All that I will tell you is, that the Duke hath dined. Get your apparel together; good strings to your beards, new ribbons to your pumps; meet presently at the palace; every man look over his part; for the short and the long is, our play is preferred. In any case, let Thisbe have clean linen; and let not him that plays the lion pare his nails, for they shall hang out for the lion's claws. And, most dear actors, eat no onions nor garlic, for we are to utter sweet breath; and I do not doubt but to hear them say it is a sweet comedy. No more words. Away, go, away!

[*Exeunt.*]

希波吕忒：　但他们所说的一夜间全部的经历，以及他们大家心理上都受到同样影响的一件事实，可以证明那不会是幻想。虽然那故事是怪异而惊人，却并不令人不能置信。

忒修斯：　这一班恋人们高高兴兴地来了。

（拉山德、狄米特律斯、赫米娅、海丽娜上。）

忒修斯：　恭喜，好朋友们！恭喜！愿你们心灵里永远享受着没有阴翳的爱情日子！

拉山德：　愿更大的幸福永远追随着殿下的起居！

忒修斯：　来，我们应当用什么假面剧或是舞蹈来消磨在尾餐和就寝之间的三点钟悠长岁月呢？我们一向掌管戏乐的人在哪里？有哪几种余兴准备着？有没有一出戏剧可以祛除难挨的时辰里按捺不住的焦灼呢？叫菲劳斯特莱特过来。

菲劳斯特莱特：　有，伟大的忒修斯。

忒修斯：　说，你有些什么可以缩短这黄昏的节目？有些什么假面剧？有些什么音乐？要是一点娱乐都没有，我们怎么把这迟迟

The lazy time, if not with some delight?

PHILOST.　There is a brief how many sports are ripe;

Make choice of which your Highness will see first.

[*Giving a paper.*]

THESEUS.　The battle with the Centaurs, to be sung

By an Athenian eunuch to the harp.

We'll none of that: that have I told my love,

In glory of my kinsman Hercules.

The riot of the tipsy Bacchanals,

Tearing the Thracian singer in their rage.

That is an old device, and it was played

When I from Thebes came last a conqueror.

The thrice three Muses mourning for the death

Of Learning, late deceased in beggary.

That is some satire, keen and critical,

Not sorting with a nuptial ceremony.

A tedious brief scene of young Pyramus

And his love Thisbe; very tragical mirth.

Merry and tragical! tedious and brief!

That is hot ice and wondrous strange snow.

How shall we find the concord of this discord?

PHILOST.　A play there is, my lord, some ten words long,

Which is as brief as I have known a play;

But by ten words, my lord, it is too long,

Which makes it tedious; for in all the play

There is not one word apt, one player fitted.

的时间消度过去呢？

菲劳斯特莱特：　这儿是一张预备好的各种戏目的单子，请殿下自己拣选哪一项先来。（呈上单子。）

忒修斯：　"与马人作战，由一个雅典太监和竖琴而唱"。那个我们不要听；我已经告诉过我的爱人这一段表彰我的姻兄赫剌克勒斯武功的故事了。"醉酒者之狂暴，特剌刻歌人惨遭肢裂的始末。"那是老调，当我上次征服忒拜凯旋回来的时候就已经表演过了。"九缪斯神痛悼学术的沦亡"。那是一段犀利尖刻的讽刺，不适合于婚礼时的表演。"关于年轻的皮拉摩斯及其爱人提斯柏的冗长的短戏，非常悲哀的趣剧"。悲哀的趣剧！冗长的短戏！那简直是说灼热的冰，发烧的雪。这种矛盾怎么能调和起来呢？

菲劳斯特莱特：　殿下，一出一共只有十来个字那么长的戏，当然是再短没有了；然而即使只有十个字，也会嫌太长，叫人看了厌倦；因为在全剧之中，没有一个字是用得恰当的，没有一个演员是支配得适如其份的。那本戏的确很悲哀，殿下，因为皮拉摩斯在戏里要把自己杀死。可是我看他们预演那一场的时候，

And tragical, my noble lord, it is;

For Pyramus therein doth kill himself.

Which when I saw rehearsed, I must confess,

Made mine eyes water; but more merry tears

The passion of loud laughter never shed.

THESEUS.   What are they that do play it?

PHILOST.   Hard-handed men that work in Athens here,

Which never laboured in their minds till now;

And now have toiled their unbreathed memories

With this same play against your nuptial.

THESEUS.   And we will hear it.

PHILOST.   No, my noble lord,

It is not for you. I have heard it over,

And it is nothing, nothing in the world;

Unless you can find sport in their intents,

Extremely stretched and conned with cruel pain,

To do you service.

THESEUS.   I will hear that play;

For never anything can be amiss

When simpleness and duty tender it.

Go, bring them in; and take your places, ladies.

[*Exit Philostrate.*]

HIPPOLYTA.   I love not to see wretchedness o'er-charged,

And duty in his service perishing.

我得承认确曾使我的眼中充满了眼泪；但那些泪都是在纵声大笑的时候忍俊不住而流下来的，再没有人流过比那更开心的泪水了。

忒修斯： 扮演这戏的是些什么人呢？

菲劳斯特莱特： 都是在这儿雅典城里做工过活的胖手胝足的汉子。他们从来不曾用过头脑，今番为了准备参加殿下的婚礼，才辛辛苦苦地把这本戏记诵起来。

忒修斯： 好，就让我们听一下吧。

菲劳斯特莱特： 不，殿下，那是不配烦渎您的耳朵的。我已经听完过他们一次，简直一无足取；除非你嘉纳他们的一片诚心和苦苦背诵的辛勤。

忒修斯： 我要把那本戏听一次，因为纯朴和忠诚所呈献的礼物，总是可取的。去把他们带来。各位夫人女士们，大家请坐下。

（菲劳斯特莱特下。）

希波吕忒： 我不欢喜看见微贱的人作他们力量所不及的事，忠诚因为努力的狂妄而变成毫无价值。

THESEUS.   Why, gentle sweet, you shall see no such thing.

HIPPOLYTA.   He says they can do nothing in this kind.

THESEUS.   The kinder we, to give them thanks for nothing.

> Our sport shall be to take what they mistake;
>
> And what poor duty cannot do,
>
> Noble respect takes it in might, not merit.
>
> Where I have come, great clerks have purposed
>
> To greet me with premeditated welcomes;
>
> Where I have seen them shiver and look pale,
>
> Make periods in the midst of sentences,
>
> Throttle their practised accent in their fears,
>
> And, in conclusion, dumbly have broke off,
>
> Not paying me a welcome. Trust me, sweet,
>
> Out of this silence yet I picked a welcome;
>
> And in the modesty of fearful duty
>
> I read as much as from the rattling tongue
>
> Of saucy and audacious eloquence.
>
> Love, therefore, and tongue-tied simplicity
>
> In least speak most to my capacity.

[Re-enter Philostrate.]

PHILOST.   So please your Grace, the Prologue is addressed.

THESEUS.   Let him approach.

> *[Flourish of trumpets.]*

忒修斯：　啊，亲爱的，你不会看见他们糟到那地步。

希波吕忒：　他说他们根本不会演戏。

忒修斯：　那更显得我们的宽宏大度，虽然他们的劳力毫无价值，他们仍能得到我们的嘉纳。我们可以把他们的错误作为取笑的资料。我们不必较量他们那可怜的忠诚所不能达到的成就，而该重视他们的辛勤。凡是我所到的地方，那些有学问的人都预先准备好欢迎辞迎接我；但是一看见了我，便发抖、脸色变白，句子没有说完便中途顿住，背熟了的话梗在喉中，吓得说不出来，结果是一句欢迎我的话都没有说。相信我，亲爱的，从这种无言中我却领受了他们一片欢迎的诚意；在诚惶诚恐的忠诚的畏怯上表示出来的意味，并不少于一条娓娓动听的辩舌和无所忌惮的口才。因此，爱人，照我所能观察到的，无言的纯朴所表示的情感，才是最丰富的。

（菲劳斯特莱特重上。）

菲劳斯特莱特：　请殿下吩咐，念开场诗的预备登场了。

忒修斯：　让他上来吧。

（喇叭奏花腔。）

[*Enter Quince as the Prologue.*]

PROLOG.　If we offend, it is with our good will.

　　That you should think, we come not to offend,

　　But with good will. To show our simple skill,

　　That is the true beginning of our end.

　　Consider then, we come but in despite.

　　We do not come, as minding to content you,

　　Our true intent is. All for your delight

　　We are not here. That you should here repent you,

　　The actors are at band; and, by their show,

　　You shall know all, that you are like to know,

THESEUS.　This fellow doth not stand upon points.

LYSANDE.　He hath rid his prologue like a rough colt; he knows not

　　the stop. A good moral, my lord: it is not enough to speak, but to

　　speak true.

HIPPOLYTA.　Indeed he hath played on this prologue like a child on

　　a recorder – a sound, but not in government.

THESEUS.　His speech was like a tangled chain; nothing impaired,

　　but all disordered. Who is next?

[*Enter Pyramus and Thisbe, Wall, Moonshine, and Lion.*]

PROLOG.　Gentles, perchance you wonder at this show;

　　But wonder on, till truth make all things plain.

（昆斯上，念开场诗。）

昆斯：　要是咱们，得罪了请原谅。

　　　　咱们本来是，一片的好意，

　　　　想要显一显。薄薄的伎俩，

　　　　那才是咱们原来的本意。

　　　　因此列位咱们到这儿来。

　　　　为的要让列位欢笑欢笑，

　　　　否则就是不曾。到这儿来，

　　　　如果咱们。惹动列位气恼。

　　　　一个个演员，都将，要登场，

　　　　你们可以仔细听个端详。[1]

忒修斯：　这家伙简直乱来。

拉山德：　他念他的开场诗就像骑一头顽劣的小马一样，乱冲乱撞，
　　　　该停的地方不停，不该停的地方偏偏停下。殿下，这是一个好
　　　　教训：单是会讲话不能算数，要讲话总该讲得像个路数。

希波吕忒：　真的，他就像一个小孩子学吹笛，呜哩呜哩了一下，
　　　　可是全不入调。

忒修斯：　他的话像是一段纠缠在一起的链索，并没有欠缺，可是
　　　　全弄乱了。跟着是谁登场呢？

（皮拉摩斯及提斯柏、墙、月光、狮子上。）

昆斯：　列位大人，也许你们会奇怪这一班人跑出来干么。尽管奇

---

[1] 此段译文标点还有待斟酌。

This man is Pyramus, if you would know;

This beauteous lady Thisbe is certain.

This man, with lime and rough-cast, doth present

Wall, that vile Wall which did these lovers sunder;

And through Walls chink, poor souls, they are content

To whisper. At the which let no man wonder.

This man, with lanthorn, dog, and bush of thorn,

Presenteth Moonshine; for, if you will know,

By moonshine did these lovers think no scorn

To meet at Ninus' tomb, there, there to woo.

This grisly beast, which Lion hight by name,

The trusty Thisbe, coming first by night,

Did scare away, or rather did affright;

And as she fled, her mantle she did fall;

Which Lion vile with bloody mouth did stain.

Anon comes Pyramus, sweet youth and tall,

And finds his trusty Thisbe's mantle slain;

Whereat with blade, with bloody blameful blade,

He bravely broached his boiling bloody breast;

And Thisbe, tarrying in mulberry shade,

His dagger drew, and died. For all the rest,

Let Lion, Moonshine, Wall, and lovers twain,

At large discourse while here they do remain.

[*Exeunt Prologue, Pyramus, Thisbe, Lion, and Moonshine.*]

THESEUS.   I wonder if the lion be to speak.

怪吧，自然而然地你们总会明白过来。这个人是皮拉摩斯，要
是你们想要知道的话；这位美丽的姑娘不用说便是提斯柏啦。
这个人身上涂着石灰和黏土，是代表墙头的，那堵隔开这两个
情人的坏墙头；他们这两个可怜的人只好在墙缝里低声谈话，
这是要请大家明白的。这个人提着灯笼，牵着犬，拿着柴枝，
是代表月亮；因为你们要知道，这两个情人觉得在月光底下到
尼纳斯的坟头见面谈情倒也不坏。这一头可怕的畜生名叫狮子，
那晚上忠实的提斯柏先到约会的地方，给它吓跑了，或者不如
说是被它惊走了；她在逃走的时候脱落了她的外套，那件外套
因为给那恶狮子咬住在它那张血嘴里，所以沾满了血斑。隔了
不久，皮拉摩斯，那个高个儿的美少年，也来了，一见他那忠
实的提斯柏的外套躺在地上死了，便赤楞楞地一声拔出一把血
淋淋的该死的剑来，对准他那热辣辣的胸脯里豁拉拉地刺了进
去。那时提斯柏却躲在桑树的树荫里，等到她发现了这回事，
便把他身上的剑拔出来，结果了她自己的性命。至于其余的一
切，可以让狮子、月光、墙头和两个情人详详细细地告诉你们，
当他们上场的时候。

（昆斯及皮拉摩斯、提斯柏、狮子、月光同下。）

忒修斯：　我不知道狮子要不要说话。

DEMETR.　No wonder, my lord: one lion may, when many asses do.

WALL.　In this same interlude it doth befall

That I, one Snout by name, present a wall;

And such a wall as I would have you think

That had in it a crannied hole or chink,

Through which the lovers, Pyramus and Thisbe,

Did whisper often very secretly.

This loam, this rough-cast, and this stone, doth show

That I am that same wall; the truth is so;

And this the cranny is, right and sinister,

Through which the fearful lovers are to whisper.

THESEUS.　Would you desire lime and hair to speak better?

DEMETR.　It is the wittiest partition that ever I heard discourse, my lord.

THESEUS.　Pyramus draws near the wall; silence.

[*Enter Pyramus.*]

PYRAMU.　O grim-looked night! O night with hue so black!

O night, which ever art when day is not!

O night, O night, alack, alack, alack,

I fear my Thisbe's promise is forgot!

And thou, O wall, O sweet, O lovely wall,

That stand'st between her father's ground and mine;

Thou wall, O wall, O sweet and lovely wall,

Show me thy chink, to blink through with mine eyne.

狄米特律斯： 殿下，这可不用怀疑，要是一班驴子都会讲人话，狮子当然也会说话啦。

墙： 小子斯诺特是也，在这本戏文里扮作墙头；须知此墙不是他墙，乃是一堵有裂缝的墙，凑着那条裂缝，皮拉摩斯和提斯柏两个情人常常偷偷地低声谈话。这一把石灰、这一撮黏土、这一块砖头，表明咱是一堵真正的墙头，并非滑头冒牌之流。这便是那条从右到左的缝儿，这两个胆小的情人就在那儿谈着知心话儿。

忒修斯： 石灰和泥土筑成的东西，居然这样会说话，难得难得！

狄米特律斯： 殿下，我从来也不曾听见过一堵墙居然能说出这样俏皮的话来。

忒修斯： 皮拉摩斯走近墙边来了。静听！

（皮拉摩斯重上。）

皮拉摩斯： 板着脸孔的夜啊！漆黑的夜啊！

夜啊，白天一去，你就来啦！

夜啊！夜啊！唉呀！唉呀！唉呀！

咱担心咱的提斯柏要失约啦！

墙啊！亲爱的、可爱的墙啊！

你硬生生地隔开了咱们两人的家！

墙啊！亲爱的，可爱的墙啊！

露出你的裂缝，让咱向里头瞧瞧吧！

[*Wall holds up his fingers.*]

Thanks, courteous wall. Jove shield thee well for this!

But what see what see I? No Thisbe do I see.

O wicked wall, through whom I see no bliss,

Cursed he thy stones for thus deceiving me!

THESEUS.   The wall, methinks, being sensible, should curse again.

PYRAMU.   No, in truth, sir, he should not. Deceiving me is Thisbe's

cue. She is to enter now, and I am to spy her through the wall.

You shall see it will fall pat as I told you; yonder she comes.

[*Enter Thisbe.*]

THISBE.   O wall, full often hast thou beard my moans,

For parting my fair Pyramus and me!

My cherry lips have often kissed thy stones,

Thy stones with lime and hair knit up in thee.

PYRAMU.   I see a voice; now will I to the chink,

To spy an I can hear my Thisbe's face.

Thisbe!

THISBE.   My love! thou art my love, I think.

PYRAMU.   Think what thou wilt, I am thy lover's grace;

And like Limander am I trusty still.

THISBE.   And I like Helen, till the Fates me kill.

PYRAMU.   Not Shafalus to Procrus was so true.

THISBE.   As Shafalus to Procrus, I to you.

PYRAMU.   O, kiss me through the hole of this vile wall.

（墙举手叠指作裂缝状。）

　　谢谢你，殷勤的墙！上帝大大保佑你！

　　但是咱瞧见些什么呢？咱瞧不见伊。

　　刁恶的墙啊！不让咱瞧见可爱的伊；

　　愿你倒霉吧，因为你竟这样把咱欺！

忒修斯：　这墙并不是没有知觉的，我想他应当反骂一下。

皮拉摩斯：　没有的事，殿下，真的，他不能。"把咱欺"是该提

　　斯柏接下去的尾白；她现在就要上场啦，咱就要在墙缝里看她。

　　你们瞧着吧，下面做下去正跟咱告诉你们的完全一样。那边她

　　来啦。

（提斯柏重上。）

提泰妮娅：　墙啊！你常常听得见咱的呻吟，

　　怨你生生把咱共他两两分拆！

　　咱的樱唇常跟你的砖石亲吻，

　　你那用泥泥胶得紧紧的砖石。

皮拉摩斯：　咱瞧见一个声音；让咱去望望，

　　不知可能听见提斯柏的脸庞。

　　提斯柏！

提泰妮娅：　你是咱的好人儿，咱想。

皮拉摩斯：　尽你想吧，咱是你风流的情郎。

　　好像里芒德，咱此心永无变更。

提泰妮娅：　咱就像海伦，到死也决不变心。

皮拉摩斯：　沙发勒斯对待普洛克勒斯不过如此。

提泰妮娅：　你就是普洛克勒斯，咱就是沙发勒斯。

皮拉摩斯：　啊，在这堵万恶的墙缝中请给咱一吻！

THISBE.   I kiss the wall's hole, not your lips at all.

PYRAMU.   Wilt thou at Ninny's tomb meet me straightway?

THISBE.   Tide life, tide death, I come without delay.

[*Exeunt Pyramus and Thisbe.*]

WALL.   Thus have I, Wall, my part discharged so;

    And, being done, thus Wall away doth go.

    [*Exit Wall.*]

THESEUS.   Now is the moon used between the two neighbours.

DEMETR.   No remedy, my lord, when walls are so wilful to hear without warning.

HIPPOLYTA.   This is the silliest stuff that ever I heard.

THESEUS.   The best in this kind are but shadows; and the worst are no worse, if imagination amend them.

HIPPOLYTA.   It must be your imagination then, and not theirs.

THESEUS.   If we imagine no worse of them than they of themselves, they may pass for excellent men. Here come two noble beasts in, a man and a lion.

[*Enter Lion and Moonshine.*]

LION.   You, ladies, you, whose gentle hearts do fear

    The smallest monstrous mouse that creeps on floor,

    May now, perchance, both quake and tremble here,

提泰妮娅：　咱吻着墙缝，可全然吻不到你的嘴唇。

皮拉摩斯：　你肯不肯到宁尼的坟头去跟咱相聚？

提泰妮娅：　活也好，死也好，咱一准立刻动身前去。

（二人下。）

墙：　现在咱已把墙头扮好，

　　　因此咱便要拔脚跑了。

　　　（下。）

忒修斯：　现在隔在这两份人家之间的墙头已经倒下了。

狄米特律斯：　殿下，墙头要是都像这样随随便便偷听人家的谈话，可真没法好想。

希波吕忒：　我从来没有听到过比这再蠢的东西。

忒修斯：　最好的戏剧也不过是人生的一个缩影；最坏的只要用想象补足一下，也就不会坏到什么地方去。

希波吕忒：　那该是靠你的想象，而不是靠他们的想象。

忒修斯：　要是他们在我们的想象里并不比在他们自己的想象里更坏，那么他们也可以算得顶好的人了。两个好东西登场了，一个是人，一个是狮子。

（狮子及月光重上。）

狮子：　各位太太小姐们，你们那柔弱的心一见了地板上爬着的一头顶小的老鼠就会害怕，现在看见一头凶暴的狮子发狂地怒吼，多少要发起抖来吧？但是请你们放心，咱实在是细木工匠斯纳

When lion rough in wildest rage doth roar.

Then know that I as Snug the joiner am

A lion fell, nor else no lion's dam;

For, if I should as lion come in strife

Into this place, 'twere pity on my life.

THESEUS.　A very gentle beast, and of a good conscience.

DEMETR.　The very best at a beast, my lord, that e'er I saw.

LYSANDE.　This lion is a very fox for his valour.

THESEUS.　True; and a goose for his discretion.

DEMETR.　Not so, my lord; for his valour cannot carry his discretion, and the fox carries the goose.

THESEUS.　His discretion, I am sure, cannot carry his valour; for the goose carries not the fox. It is well. Leave it to his discretion, and let us listen to the Moon.

MOON.　This lanthorn doth the horned moon present –

DEMETR.　He should have worn the horns on his head.

THESEUS.　He is no crescent, and his horns are invisible within the circumference.

MOON.　This lanthorn doth the horned moon present;

Myself the Man in the Moon do seem to be.

THESEUS.　This is the greatest error of all the rest; the man should be put into the lantern. How is it else the man in the moon?

DEMETR.　He dares not come there for the candle; for, you see, it is already in snuff.

HIPPOLYTA.　I am aweary of this moon. Would he would change!

THESEUS.　It appears, by his small light of discretion, that he is in

格，既不是凶猛的公狮，也不是一头母狮；要是咱真的是一头
狮子冲到了这儿，那咱才大倒其霉！

忒修斯： 一头非常善良的畜生，有一颗好良心。

狄米特律斯： 殿下，这是我所看见过的最好的畜生了。

拉山德： 这头狮子按勇气说只好算是一只狐狸。

忒修斯： 对了，而且按他那小心翼翼的样子说起来倒像是一头鹅。

狄米特律斯： 可不能那么说，殿下；因为他的"勇气"还敌不过
他的"小心"，可是一头狐狸却能把一头鹅拖了走。

忒修斯： 我肯定说，他的"小心"推不动他的"勇气"，就像一
头鹅拖不动一头狐狸。好，别管他吧，让我们听月亮说话。

月光： 这盏灯笼代表着角儿弯弯的新月；——

狄米特律斯： 他应当把角装在头上。

忒修斯： 他并不是新月，圆圆的哪里有个角儿？

月光： 这盏灯笼代表着角儿弯弯的新月；咱好像就是月亮里的仙
人。

忒修斯： 这该是最大的错误了。应该把这个人放进灯笼里去；否
则他怎么会是月亮里的仙人呢？

狄米特律斯： 他因为怕烛火要恼火，所以不敢进去。

希波吕忒： 这月亮真使我厌倦；他应该变化变化才好！

忒修斯： 照他那昏昏沉沉的样子看起来，他大概是一个残月；但

the wane; but yet, in courtesy, in all reason, we must stay the time.

LYSANDE.   Proceed, Moon.

MOON.   All that I have to say is to tell you that the lanthorn is the moon; I, the Man in the Moon; this thorn-bush, my thorn-bush; and this dog, my dog.

DEMETR.   Why, all these should be in the lantern; for all these are in the moon. But silence; here comes Thisbe.

[*Re-enter Thisbe.*]

THISBE.   This is old Ninny's tomb. Where is my love?

LION.   [*Roaring*] Oh!

　　　[*Thisbe runs off.*]

DEMETR.   Well roared, Lion.

THESEUS.   Well run, Thisbe.

HIPPOLYTA.   Well shone, Moon. Truly, the moon shines with a good grace.

　　　[*The Lion tears Thisbe's Mantle.*]

THESEUS.   Well moused, Lion.

DEMETR.   And then came Pyramus.

LYSANDE.   And so the lion vanished.

[*Enter Pyramus.*]

PYRAMU.   Sweet Moon, I thank thee for thy sunny beams;

是为着礼貌和一切的理由，我们得忍耐一下。

拉山德：　说下去，月亮。

月光：　总而言之，咱要告诉你们的是，这灯笼便是月亮；咱便是
　　　月亮里的仙人；这柴枝是咱的柴枝；这狗是咱的狗。

狄米特律斯：　嗨，这些都应该放进灯笼里去才对，因为它们都是
　　　在月亮里的。但是静些，提斯柏来了。

（提斯柏重上。）

提泰妮娅：　这是宁尼老人的坟。咱的好人儿呢？

狮子：　（吼）呜！——（提斯柏奔下。）

狄米特律斯：　吼得好，狮子！

忒修斯：　奔得好，提斯柏！

希波吕忒：　照得好，月亮！真的，月亮照得姿势很好。

（狮子撕破提斯柏的外套后下。）

忒修斯：　撕得好，狮子！

狄米特律斯：　于是皮拉摩斯来了。

拉山德：　于是狮子不见了。

（皮拉摩斯重上。）

皮拉摩斯：　可爱的月亮，咱多谢你的阳光；

I thank thee, Moon, for shining now so bright;

For, by thy gracious golden, glittering gleams,

I trust to take of truest Thisbe sight.

But stay, O spite!

But mark, poor knight,

What dreadful dole is here!

Eyes, do you see?

How can it be?

O dainty duck! O dear!

Thy mantle good,

What! stained with blood?

Approach, ye Furies fell.

O Fates! come, come;

Cut thread and thrum;

Quail, crush, conclude, and quell.

THESEUS.　This passion, and the death of a dear friend, would go near to make a man look sad.

HIPPOLYTA.　Beshrew my heart, but I pity the man.

PYRAMU.　O wherefore, Nature, didst thou lions frame?

Since lion vile hath here deflowered my dear;

Which is – no, no – which was the fairest dame

That lived, that loved, that liked, that looked with cheer.

Come, tears, confound;

Out, sword, and wound

The pap of Pyramus;

Ay, that left pap,

　　谢谢你，因为你照得这么皎洁！

　　靠着你那慈和的闪烁的金光，

　　咱将要饱餐着提斯柏的秀色。

　　但是且住，啊该死！

　　瞧哪，可怜的骑士，

　　这是一场什么惨景！

　　眼睛，你看不看见？

　　这种事怎会出现？

　　可爱的宝贝啊，亲亲！

　　你的好外套一件，

　　怎么全都是血点？

　　过来吧，狰狞的凶神！

　　快把生命的羁缠

　　从此后一刀割断；

　　今朝咱了结了残生！

忒修斯：　这一种情感再加上一个好朋友的死，很可以使一个人脸
　　　　　带愁容。

希波吕忒：　该死！我倒真有点可怜这个人。

皮拉摩斯：　苍天啊！你为什么要造下狮子，

　　　　　让它在这里蹂躏了咱的爱人？

　　　　　她在一切活着爱着的人中，

　　　　　是一个最美最美最最美的美人。

　　　　　淋漓地流吧，眼泪！

　　　　　咱要把宝剑一挥，

　　　　　当着咱的胸头划破：

　　　　　一剑刺过了左胸，

Where heart doth hop.

Thus die I, thus, thus, thus.

[*Stabs himself.*]

Now am I dead,

Now am I fled;

My soul is in the sky.

Tongue, lose thy light;

Moon, take thy flight.

[*Exit Moonshine.*]

Now die, die, die, die, die.

[*Dies –*]

DEMETR.   No die, but an ace, for him; for he is but one.

LYSANDE.   Less than an ace, man; for he is dead; he is nothing.

THESEUS.   With the help of a surgeon he might yet recover and yet prove an ass.

HIPPOLYTA.   How chance Moonshine is gone before Thisbe comes back and finds her lover?

THESEUS.   She will find him by starlight. Here she comes; and her passion ends the play.

[*Re-enter Thisbe.*]

HIPPOLYTA.   Methinks she should not use a long one for such a Pyramus; I hope she will be brief.

DEMETR.   A mote will turn the balance, which Pyramus, which Thisbe, is the better – he for a man,

叫心儿莫再跳动，

这样咱就死啰死啰！

（以剑自刺。）

现在咱已经身死，

现在咱已经去世，

咱灵魂儿升到天堂；

太阳，不要再照耀！

月亮，给咱拔脚跑！

（月光下。）

咱已一命、一命丧亡。

（死。）

狄米特律斯：　不是双亡，是单亡，因为他是孤零零地死去。

拉山德：　他现在死去，不但成不了双，而且成不了单；他已经变成"没有"啦。

忒修斯：　要是就去请外科医生来，也许还可以把他医活转来，叫他做一头驴子。

希波吕忒：　提斯柏还要回来找她的情人，月亮怎么这样性急，这会儿就走了呢？

忒修斯：　她可以在星光底下看见他的，现在她来了。她再痛哭流涕一下子，戏文也就完了。

（提斯柏重上。）

希波吕忒：　我想对于这样一个宝货皮拉摩斯，她可以不必浪费口舌；我希望她说得短一点儿。

狄米特律斯：　她跟皮拉摩斯较量起来真是半斤八两。上帝保佑我们不要嫁到这种男人，也保佑我们不要娶着这种妻子！

God warrant us: She for a woman, God bless us!

LYSANDE.　She hath spied him already with those sweet eyes.

DEMETR.　And thus she moans, videlicet: –

THISBE.　Asleep, my love?

What, dead, my dove?

O Pyramus, arise,

Speak, speak. Quite dumb?

Dead, dead? A tomb

Must cover thy sweet eyes.

These lily lips,

This cherry nose,

These yellow cowslip cheeks,

Are gone, are gone;

Lovers, make moan;

His eyes were green as leeks.

O Sisters Three,

Come, come to me,

With hands as pale as milk;

Lay them in gore,

Since you have shore

With shears his thread of silk.

Tongue, not a word.

Come, trusty sword;

Come, blade, my breast imbrue.

[*Stabs herself.*]

And farewell, friends;

拉山德：　她那秋波已经看见他了。

狄米特律斯：　于是悲声而言曰：——

提泰妮娅：　睡着了吗，好人儿？

　　啊！死了，咱的鸽子？

　　皮拉摩斯啊，快醒醒！

　　说呀！说呀！哑了吗？

　　唉，死了！一堆黄沙

　　将要盖住你的美睛。

　　嘴唇像百合花开，

　　鼻子像樱桃可爱，

　　黄花像是你的脸孔，

　　一齐消失、消失了，

　　有情人同声哀悼！

　　他眼睛绿得像青葱。

　　命运女神三姊妹，

　　快快到我这里来，

　　伸出你玉手像白面，

　　伸进血里泡一泡——

　　既然克擦一剪刀，

　　你割断他的生命线。

　　舌头，不许再多言！

　　凭着这一柄好剑，

　　赶快把咱胸膛刺穿。

　　（以剑自刺。）

　　再会，我的朋友们！

Thus Thisbe ends;

Adieu, adieu, adieu.

[*Dies.*]

THESEUS.　Moonshine and Lion are left to bury the dead.

DEMETR.　Ay, and Wall too.

BOTTOM.　[*Starting up.*] No, I assure you; the wall is down that parted their fathers. Will it please you to see the Epilogue, or to hear a Bergomask dance between two of our company?

THESEUS.　No epilogue, I pray you; for your play needs no excuse. Never excuse; for when the players are all dead there need none to be blamed.

Marry, if he that writ it had played Pyramus, and hanged himself in Thisbe's garter, it would have been a fine tragedy.

And so it is, truly; and very notably discharged. But come, your Bergomask; let your epilogue alone.

[*A dance.*]

The iron tongue of midnight hath told twelve.

Lovers, to bed; 'tis almost fairy time.

I fear we shall out-sleep the coming morn,

As much as we this night have overwatched.

This palpable-gross play hath well beguiled

The heavy gait of night. Sweet friends, to bed.

A fortnight hold we this solemnity,

In nightly revels and new jollity.

[*Exeunt.*]

提斯柏已经毙命；

再见吧，再见吧，再见！

（死。）

忒修斯：　他们的葬事要让月亮和狮子来料理了吧？

狄米特律斯：　是的，还有墙头。

波顿：　（跳起。）不，咱对你们说，那堵隔开他们两家的墙早已经倒了。你们要不要瞧瞧收场诗，或者听一场咱们两个伙计的贝格摩舞？

忒修斯：　请把收场诗免了吧，因为你们的戏剧无须再请求人家原谅；扮戏的人一个个死了，我们还能责怪谁不成？真的，要是写那本戏的人自己来扮皮拉摩斯，把他自己吊死在提斯柏的袜带上，那倒真是一出绝妙的悲剧。实在你们这次演得很不错。现在把你们的收场诗搁在一旁，还是跳起你们的贝格摩舞来吧。（跳舞。）夜钟已经敲过了十二点；恋人们，睡觉去吧，现在已经差不多是神仙们游戏的时间了。我担心我们明天早晨会起不来，因为今天晚上睡得太迟。这出粗劣的戏剧却使我们不觉把冗长的时间打发走了。好朋友们，去睡吧。我们要用半月工夫把这喜庆延续，夜夜有不同的欢乐。

（众下。）

ACT V   SCENE II

[*Enter Puck.*]

PUCK.   Now the hungry lion roars,

And the wolf behowls the moon;

Whilst the heavy ploughman snores,

All with weary task fordone.

Now the wasted brands do glow,

Whilst the screech-owl, screeching loud,

Puts the wretch that lies in woe

In remembrance of a shroud.

Now it is the time of night

That the graves, all gaping wide,

Every one lets forth his sprite,

In the church-way paths to glide.

And we fairies, that do run

By the triple Hecate's team

From the presence of the sun,

Following darkness like a dream,

Now are frolic. Not a mouse

Shall disturb this hallowed house.

I am sent with broom before,

第五幕　第二场

（迫克上。）

迫克：　　饿狮在高声咆哮；

　　　　　豺狼在向月长嗥；

　　　　　农夫们鼾息沉沉，

　　　　　完毕一天的辛勤。

　　　　　火把还留着残红，

　　　　　鸱鸮叫得人胆战，

　　　　　传进愁人的耳中，

　　　　　仿佛见殓衾飘飐。

　　　　　现在夜已经深深，

　　　　　坟墓都裂开大口，

　　　　　吐出了百千幽灵，

　　　　　荒野里四散奔走。

　　　　　我们跟着赫卡忒[1]，

　　　　　离开了阳光赫奕，

　　　　　像一场梦景幽凄，

　　　　　追随黑暗的踪迹。

　　　　　且把这吉屋打扫，

　　　　　供大家一场欢闹；

---

[1] 赫卡忒（Hecate），希腊神话中的夜之女神。她是世界的缔造者之一，创造了地狱。

To sweep the dust behind the door.

[*Enter Oberon and Titania, with all their train.*]

OBERON.   Through the house give glimmering light,

By the dead and drowsy fire;

Every elf and fairy sprite

Hop as light as bird from brier;

And this ditty, after me,

Sing and dance it trippingly.

TITANIA.   First, rehearse your song by rote,

To each word a warbling note;

Hand in hand, with fairy grace,

Will we sing, and bless this place.

[*Song and dance.*]

OBERON.   Now, until the break of day,

Through this house each fairy stray.

To the best bride-bed will we,

Which by us shall blessed be;

And the issue there create

Ever shall be fortunate.

So shall all the couples three

Ever true in loving be;

And the blots of Nature's hand

Shall not in their issue stand;

Never mole, hare-lip, nor scar,

　　　　驱走扰人的小鼠，

　　　　还得揩干净门户。

（奥布朗、提泰妮娅及侍从等上。）

奥布朗：　屋中消沉的火星

　　　　微微地尚在闪耀；

　　　　跳跃着每个精灵

　　　　像花枝上的小鸟；

　　　　随我唱一支曲调，

　　　　一齐轻轻地舞蹈。

提泰妮娅：　先要把歌儿练熟，

　　　　每个字玉润珠圆；

　　　　然后齐声唱祝福，

　　　　手携手缥缈回旋。

　　　　（歌舞。）

奥布朗：　趁东方尚未发白，

　　　　让我们满屋溜达；

　　　　先去看一看新床，

　　　　祝福它吉利祯祥。

　　　　这三对新婚伉俪，

　　　　愿他们永无离贰；

　　　　生下男孩和女娃，

　　　　无妄无灾福气大；

　　　　一个个相貌堂堂，

　　　　没有一点儿破相；

　　　　不生黑痣不缺唇，

Nor mark prodigious, such as are

Despised in nativity,

Shall upon their children be.

With this field-dew consecrate,

Every fairy take his gate,

And each several chamber bless,

Through this palace, with sweet peace;

Ever shall in safety rest.

And the owner of it blest

Trip away; make no stay;

Meet me all by break of day.

[*Exeunt all but Puck.*]

PUCK.   If we shadows have offended,

Think but this, and all is mended,

That you have but slumbered here

While these visions did appear.

And this weak and idle theme,

No more yielding but a dream,

Gentles, do not reprehend.

If you pardon, we will mend.

And, as I am an honest Puck,

If we have unearned luck

Now to scape the serpent's tongue,

We will make amends ere long;

更没有半点瘢痕。
凡是不祥的胎记，
不会在身上发现。
用这神圣的野露，
永享着福禄康宁。
你们去浇洒门户，
祝福屋子的主人，
快快去，莫犹豫；
天明时我们重聚。

（除迫克外皆下。）

迫克：　要是我们这辈影子
　　　　有拂了诸位的尊意，
　　　　就请你们这样思量，
　　　　一切便可得到补偿；
　　　　这种种幻景的显现，
　　　　不过是梦中的妄念；
　　　　这一段无聊的情节，
　　　　真同诞梦一样无力。
　　　　先生们，请不要见笑！
　　　　倘蒙原宥，定当补报。
　　　　万一我们幸而免脱
　　　　这一遭嘘嘘的指斥，

Else the Puck a liar call.

So, good night unto you all.

Give me your hands, if we be friends,

And Robin shall restore amends.

[*Exit.*]

(THE END)

我们决不忘记大恩，

迫克生平不会骗人。

否则尽管骂我混蛋。

我迫克祝大家晚安。

再会了！肯赏个脸儿的话，

就请拍两下手，多谢多谢！

（下。）

（完）

中英对照全译本系列书目表

英国文学卷

《简爱》

《傲慢与偏见》

《理智与情感》

《爱玛》

《金银岛》

《呼啸山庄》

《双城记》

《雾都孤儿》

《柳林风声》

《鲁滨逊漂流记》

《一九八四 动物庄园》

《福尔摩斯经典探案集 血字的研究 四签名》

《福尔摩斯经典探案集 巴斯克维尔的猎犬 恐怖谷》

《福尔摩斯经典探案集 福尔摩斯历险记》

《福尔摩斯经典探案集 福尔摩斯回忆录》

《福尔摩斯经典探案集 福尔摩斯归来记》

《福尔摩斯经典探案集 最后的致意》

《福尔摩斯经典探案集 福尔摩斯新探案集》

《培根散文集》

《德伯家的苔丝》

《格列佛游记》

《道林·格雷的画像》

《消失的地平线》

《艰难时世》

美国文学卷

《红字》

《小妇人》

《伟大的盖茨比》

《瓦尔登湖》

《房龙地理》

《纯真年代》

《秘密花园》

《嘉莉妹妹》

《人类的故事》

《老人与海》

《太阳照常升起》

《乞力马扎罗的雪 海明威短篇小说选》

《哈克贝利·费恩历险记》

《马克·吐温短篇小说选集》

《汤姆·索亚历险记》

《欧·亨利短篇小说选集》

《本杰明·富兰克林自传》

《爱伦·坡短篇小说选》

《杰克·伦敦小说选 野性的呼唤 海狼》

《小公主》

《永别了，武器》

《丧钟为谁而鸣》

《海明威作品选》

欧洲文学卷

《茶花女》

《高老头》

《欧也妮·葛朗台》

《羊脂球 莫泊桑短篇小说选》

《包法利夫人》

《海底两万里》

《木偶奇遇记》

《爱的教育》

《地心游记》

《八十天环游地球》

《少年维特之烦恼》

《名人传》

《变色龙 契诃夫短篇小说选》

《青鸟 蜜蜂的生活》

《尼尔斯骑鹅旅行记》

《尼尔斯骑鹅旅行记：续集》

《玩偶之家》

其他文学卷

《绿山墙的安妮》

《泰戈尔诗歌集 新月集&飞鸟集》

严复译文卷

《国富论（上）》

《国富论（下）》

《天演论》

《论自由》

《社会学研究》

朱生豪译文卷

《罗密欧与朱丽叶》

《威尼斯商人》

《仲夏夜之梦》

《第十二夜》

《皆大欢喜》

《无事生非》

《哈姆莱特》

《李尔王》

《麦克白》

《奥瑟罗》